GEORGE   MEREDITH

GEORGE MEREDITH

A Primer to the Novels

BY

JAMES MOFFATT

KENNIKAT PRESS
Port Washington, N. Y./London

TO

ANY WHO DESIRE TO JOIN
"THAT ACUTE AND HONOURABLE
MINORITY WHICH CONSENTS TO BE
THWACKED WITH APHORISMS AND
SENTENCES AND A FANTASTIC
DELIVERY OF THE VERITIES."

GEORGE MEREDITH

First published 1909
Reissued in 1969 by Kennikat Press
Library of Congress Catalog Card No: 72-86044
SBN 8046-0628-5

Manufactured by Taylor Publishing Company   Dallas, Texas

Contents

v

Preface

THE object of this primer is to help some readers of Meredith over the fence. A brief sketch of his general aims and method has been prefixed, but any exposition of his cardinal ideas must be sought elsewhere. All that has been attempted in these pages is to tell, in the bare outline of a reporter's column, the exact course of the story and the precise facts of the narrative underlying each novel. Meredith's style and execution often render it rather a difficult matter for the general reader to make out what has happened or what is happening ; even when his manner is not round-about or riddling, it is frequently elusive, and hardly any of the novels, I think, will be the worse for such a plain summary of its framework as this primer tries to furnish. I have therefore printed an analysis of each, adding a note or two upon the contents and construction. From this descriptive report

Preface

the reader can pass on to enjoy the bright and bracing philosophy inside the story or to apply the principles of literary criticism.

After some hesitation I have decided to treat the novels in chronological order. They might be grouped together, but upon the whole the advantage seems to lie with an arrangement of them in the order in which they were written and published.

Introduction.

ABOUT the middle of last century a shrewd American sat down to record some impressions of our English character which he had received during a recent visit to this island. He closed his chapter upon literature with the comfortable reflection that after all some retrieving power lay in the English race, which would eventually produce a recoil from the limitations of "a self-conceited, modish life, clinging to a corporeal civilization," beefy, mechanical, and averse to ideas. Like a genuine Platonist, Emerson recollected that there were two nations in England : not the Normans and the Saxons, not Celt and Goth, not the rich and the poor, but "the perceptive class and the practical finality class." There was the nation of genius, perhaps amounting to a dozen souls, and there was the nation of animal force, which numbered some twenty

George Meredith

millions. It seemed to him that these different complexions or types of nature must re-
act on one another. To their interchange and
counterpoise he considered that the English
character owed a large measure of its virility.

Only three years or so after the idealist of
Concord had published his survey, the smaller
of these nations was to receive at least one
notable recruit in the person of a novelist
who was not afraid to state that he specially
wanted "the practical Englishman to settle
his muzzle in a nosebag of ideas." The year
1859 may be taken, for the sake of conven-
ience, as one of the landmarks in the English
literature of the nineteenth century. Before
it closed, Leigh Hunt, de Quincey, Hallam
and Macaulay passed away, while Thackeray
and Dickens gave to the world their evening
gifts in "The Virginians" and "A Tale of
Two Cities." Carlyle's work lay almost entirely behind him. New lights were rising.
"The Idylls of the King," Fitzgerald's
"Omar Khayyám," Mill's essay on Liberty,
"The Origin of Species," and "Adam
Bede," all published in 1859, usher in the later
period of Victorian literature. Freeman and

Introduction

Froude, Huxley and Tyndall, were just entering the arena, while Spencer was presently to follow them. "The Defence of Guenevere" had recently caught the attention of the cultured, and in the following year Swinburne was to woo deaf ears with "The Queen Mother" and "Rosamund." "Adam Bede" took the wind out of the sails of most contemporary fiction upon the serious tack, however, and among that becalmed class must be reckoned a prose romance entitled "The Ordeal of Richard Feverel." It was written by a young Londoner, hitherto known for the most part as the author of some rather unsuccessful verse and of two fantastic stories whose merit and promise had been generously recognised by the discerning few, and cordially reviewed—it is a pleasure to recall—by George Eliot herself, no fewer than three times.

It would be idle and impertinent to raise the veil which Meredith's reticence and modesty have drawn over his career. His life is in his books, though few writers have published perhaps so much and left their personalities so deeply in the shadow. Such

George Meredith

items of his biography as are relevant to this sketch can be stated very briefly. He was born in Hampshire, on the 12th of February, in the same year as Ibsen and Tolstoy, 1828, with the blood of working-people in his veins. His father was of Welsh extraction, his mother of Irish. After they separated he was educated in Germany, and it is superfluous to point out the significance of this for his intellectual development. Returning to this country in his sixteenth year, he was apprenticed unwillingly to the study of law, from which, like Dickens, he soon rolled off into literature and journalism, acting, for example, as the war-correspondent of the *Morning Post* in Italy during 1866. He first tried verse, in a simple, lyric vein. His later poetry became a more characteristic medium of utterance, but he is never pensive, or blithe, or stately for long, and, as an acute reviewer once pointed out, verse with him virtually tends to become more and more "a kind of imaginative logic, a reasoning in pictures." Meredith ultimately became a poet of almost the first rank, within certain limitations, but from the very first he was a poet

Introduction

in his prose. Yet even his early prose, immeasurably finer than his early verse, won quite an inadequate hearing. Recognition came slowly to his door, and amid depreciation and comparative neglect he had to struggle for years with actual privation. One solace in this ordeal was his friendship with a brilliant coterie of men, including James Thomson, the author of "The City of Dreadful Night," and that strange humourist, Thomas Love Peacock, whose daughter became Meredith's first wife. Holman Hunt thus describes his appearance about this time : "Of nut-brown hair and blue eyes, the perfect type of a well-bred Englishman, he stood about five feet eight." Eventually he shared the curious household organised at Chelsea by Swinburne and the two Rossettis, but four men of genius within four walls are scarcely a permanent concourse of atoms, and Meredith's stay was only shorter than that of Swinburne. His later years were mostly spent amid the Surrey hills, gladdened by the widening reputation which the years brought tardily around his name. Public appreciation of his genius was comparatively slow

George Meredith

and limited. This has been partly due to the peculiar nature of his work, partly, perhaps, to the general state of the English literary conscience when he first made his appeal to the reading public—if it be true, as Professor Saintsbury declares, that our criticism had reached a humiliating nadir between 1840 and 1860. Meredith's reception at any rate is not an isolated phenomenon; it illustrates the familiar law that contemporary criticisms of a masterpiece are often a staggering bequest to posterity. He had to row against the tide, and the effort was harder for him than for many others. His ideal of prose-fiction was in daring revolt against the conventional canons of an age which was not prepared to welcome even a consummate genius setting itself to be the exponent of life lived under restless tendencies due to the scientific movement and the ethical idealism of the period, with its sense of social responsibility and trend towards introspectiveness. He also shared the tendency of the Victorian period to be less inspired and more artistic than its predecessor, and in this way became a voice for other audiences than those found

Introduction

in the market-place. "My way," he confessed, "is like a Rhone island in the summer drought, stony, unattractive and difficult, between the two forceful streams of the unreal and the over-real. My people are actual, yet uncommon. It is the clock-work of the brain that they are directed to set in motion." Or, in another of his metaphors, he set out to make a road between Adam and Macadam, and he did so, using prose-fiction to mirror contemporary life as it lay between the animal existence and the artificial. To this task he brought imagination and penetration, flexibility of mind and a cosmopolitan freedom of outlook, gifts which were certain to prevail before long with the competent, but as certain to miss immediate or widespread favour with people who found it difficult to appreciate his methods or to sympathise with his peculiar aims.

For, however it may be rated, his work must be allowed to possess distinction. Even a casual reader can hardly fail to be impressed by its sense of power and its absence of echoes. In reach and range it breathes an originality, often a daring originality, which

7

George Meredith

differentiates it easily from previous or contemporary fiction. The influence of Richardson has been traced here and there, but taken as a whole, Meredith's work occupies a class of its own and goes back to few serious patterns. There is, indeed, more than a reminiscence of Peacock, e.g., in the fantastic element which occasionally crops up, from "The Shaving of Shagpat"—that amazingly witty burlesque of the Arabian Nights—to the weariful apologues of Delphica and the Rajah in London which disfigure that already tangled web, "One of Our Conquerors." Dr. Folliot in "Crotchet Castle" is cousin to Dr. Middleton in "The Egoist," and the idea underlying books like "Maid Marian" and "Farina" is substantially the same—an attempt to reproduce, with gentle satire, the mediæval romance of sentiment and gay adventure. The whimsical element, in "Nightmare Abbey," for example, the brilliant dialogue of "Melincourt" and "Headlong Hall," the attitude of keen and even caustic humour towards contemporary society and its foibles, the admixture of raillery and sympathy, the subservience of the love-

8

Introduction

interest to wider matters, the Rabelaisian fling,
the dash of farce, the combination of narrative and dissertation, the sense that nothing
can be too good and few things too bad to be
laughed at—these are some of the elements
common to Peacock and his distinguished son-
in-law, although the latter is exact and careful
in his use of language and free from outbursts
of boyish petulance. In the prelude to "The
Egoist," and occasionally in the rhapsodical
apostrophes and some of the ethical concep-
tions throughout the novels especially, there
are not indistinct echoes of Carlyle, for
whom, as readers of "Beauchamp's Career"
will recollect, Meredith, like Dickens had
undisguised admiration. Carlyle is one of
the few contemporary writers directly mentioned by the novelist, and the affinities of
thought and even expression between the two
writers demand rather more attention than
seems to have been as yet bestowed on them.
How much of Meredith's own succinct and
irregular style, for example, is recalled in
his famous account of "Heroes and Hero-
Worship"—"a style resembling either early
architecture or utter dilapidation, so loose and

rough it seemed ; a wind-in-the-orchard style, that tumbled down here and there an appreciable fruit with uncouth bluster ; sentences without commencements running to abrupt endings and smoke, like waves against a sea-wall . . . all the pages in a breeze, the whole book producing a kind of electrical agitation in the mind and the joints." Many a reader of Meredith has felt precisely like Nevil Beauchamp in Malta, as he read the black and bright lecturer on Heroes, "getting nibbles of golden meaning by instalments, as with a solitary pick in a very dark mine, until the illumination of an idea struck him that there was a great deal more in the book than there was in himself."

It is this volume and animation, informed by a brilliant style and imagination of a very high order, that constitutes the main title of George Meredith to literary fame. His work has been remarkably sustained and even in quality. "Richard Feverel" was pronounced by the *Times* to be "a powerful work, penetrative in its depth of insight and rich in its variety of experience." It is a remarkable piece of writing, but it is doubly remarkable

Introduction

when we consider that it was composed by a
man of thirty as his first serious romance, and
as far back as 1859. Plenty of writers possess
ability enough to secure one conspicuous
success, comparatively speaking, and there are
authors in every age who practically live upon
the reputation of a single early work. But
"Richard Feverel" was only the first blossom
of Meredith's genius. It was not tentative nor
did it exhaust the author's power. The long line
of its successors proved that he possessed
intellectual resources versatile and serious
enough to deserve the closest consideration
from anyone who would estimate the central
currents of literary influence flowing through
the Victorian era. A dozen times at least
in almost every one of his novels we stop to
say, "this is literature"; the workmanship
wears what Coventry Patmore called "the
glittering crown of wit," viz., "a synthesis of
gravity of matter and gaiety of manner."
But Meredith is more than a littérateur. There
are passages which arrest and impress the
reader with a still deeper feeling, when the
mass of thought or the thrill of action is
clothed upon with passion, and words fit

emotion with a felicitousness or a closeness which seems inevitable. At Belthorpe or at Wilming Weir, with Emilia singing in the wood, over Clare Doria Forey's diary and the marine duet in "Lord Ormont and his Aminta," with Mazzini in Italy or Beauchamp at Venice, at the cricket supper in " Evan Harrington" or with Harry and Temple on the Priscilla, with Lord Fleetwood at his prize fight and Diana Warwick at the Crossways— over these and fifty other passages, salt and aglow with the breath of reality, the pulse quickens. We forget the author, we forget the book ; the word springs to our lips, "This —this is life." The sense of style and com- position, elsewhere (it must be owned) not always unobtrusive, falls away before the consciousness of life seen and life shown. Genius is not a word to be applied broadcast, particularly among novelists, but no other term is adequate to such proofs of mental power. No doubt there are tracts in Meredith over which, more or less reasonably, people gasp and yawn, but these are trifling compared to the total achievement of the author, and it is upon the evidence of such passages as I

Introduction

have indicated that in all fairness he must be judged. A racehorse, Montaigne will tell you in his acute and charitable way, is remembered not by his defeats but by the races he has won.

If novels are to be written on a theory, it is good to have the theory expounded by the novelist himself, as by Fielding in the preface to " Joseph Andrews." Thanks to scattered hints throughout the novels, principally in defence of his hand-maiden Philosophy, as well as to the published "Essay upon Comedy," we possess sufficient points to enable us roughly to calculate the curve pursued by Meredith's vivacious, graceful genius. Take first and foremost these lines from his "Modern Love." He writes :

In tragic life, God wot,
No villain need be ! Passions spin the plot :
We are betrayed by what is false within.

The heart of Meredith's method lies in these three lines, and it is true to the Aristotelian canon. There are really no villains in his novels. The oversong of the philosophy which dominates his prose, is that character amounts to fate ; some inward twist of the

13

George Meredith

soul, some mental deviation, *that* explains the mischief done by a man to himself or others. Impulses and motives swarm in the pool of consciousness, and over that pool you find Meredith bending eagerly. It is rippled by circumstance, to be sure, but he is mainly engrossed in a minute and varied study of that "busy little creature," the human self, with its attendant infusoria of whims and passions. This was not by any means a new departure in fiction. Such a psychological attitude had been already occupied by George Eliot, whose lineal successor in this direction Meredith undoubtedly may claim to be ; and it is not perhaps insignificant that the definitive edition of the *Comédie Humaine* was published in the same year as "Richard Feverel." But *es giebt kein Plagiat in der Philosophie*, and this interest in mental chemistry is perennial. Meredith captivates his audience at any rate by quite an original application of the psychological method, combining the unconcern of the artist with something of the keen seriousness felt by a responsible thinker. He sums all this up conveniently in the phrase—"the Comic Spirit"; a hint which supplies us with

14

the colours upon his palette and the features of the one model who sits to him in all manner of positions for her portrait.

The "Comic Spirit" represents an attitude of mind to life. Contemplative passion or—better still—impassioned contemplation might be taken as its definition. It is the *ethos* of a calm, curious observer, alive to the pretences and foibles of mankind, yet loving them none the less that he is thus acutely sensitive to their untrained opinions, their affectations, pedantries, delusions, inconsistencies, hypocrisies. The Comic Spirit is incisive. But it is creative and instructive, as well as critical. It represents the wit of wisdom, sly, shrewd, and sympathetic—as we find it, for example, in Chaucer or in Shakespeare, the Shakespeare of Theseus in the "Midsummer Night's Dream" as he chides Hippolyta. In Meredith it plays upon men's motives as these are rippled by the social world. It feels for the springs of action lying in the ideas rather than in the appetites of man. Life, Meredith protests, is crossed and recrossed by people who drift into absurdities, or riot in unconscious vanities, or make pretensions, or violate indi-

15

George Meredith

vidually and in the bulk unwritten laws of justice, reason, and good sense, getting themselves into every kind of tragic or false position. The Comic Spirit traces in all this "what is false within," what pulls the strings. And its object is not malign. Really it is on the side of hope, imagination, and romance; it is never spiteful or superior. It prevents the lassitude of indifference and delivers from a bitter and mad despair. You come near defining it when you speak of "the humour of the mind," rich and warm and wise, which strives to transmute sympathy from intolerable pain into active interest, and which is pleasantly bent upon disentangling commonsense from its corruptions and from what is often worse—its caricatures.

What then is the proper field of the Comic Spirit? Evidently social life, and especially the refined and polished existence peculiar to the trim parks of modern civilisation, "where we have no dust of the struggling outer world, no mire, no violent crashes." Like his favourite poets, Menander, Terence, and Molière, Meredith is a painter of manners—manners being ultimately *mores*. He

16

Introduction

is deeply concerned with the qualities and conditions of contemporary society, the marsh where the plant of his quest grows luxuriantly. Man's future on earth, he is frank to confess, does not concern the Comic Spirit; but man's honesty and shapeliness in the present does. To Meredith, accordingly, the state of English society with its mental lethargy, is a fair province for the exercise of his analysis. "The English," we read, "are people requiring to be studied, who mean well, and are warm somewhere below, as chimney-pots are, though they are so stiff." "They call themselves practical for having an addiction to the palpable." This applies mainly to the upper classes; for although Meredith hardly ever fails in depicting country folk or vulgar natures, these are foils as a rule to the leading figures, and his method naturally leads him to find his central pivots elsewhere. He succeeds, where Dickens failed, with his aristocrats. Over and again his microscope is turned upon the British aristocracy or upper middle class, not seldom (like the Matthew Arnold of "Culture and Anarchy") upon young gentlemen "who are

17

B

simply engines of their appetites and to the philosophic eye" quite savage and primeval. His backgrounds range from Wales to Italy; German socialism, the Italian or Spanish War of Independence, English politics, mining, education, railways, the navy—anything to throw into relief the pettiness of luxury, whether luxury means the wrapping up of the mind or the indulgence of the appetites. It is noticeable, too, that he is fond of introducing some conflict and play of different temperaments, either social or racial, English or foreign ; for example, Celtic and Italian, Radical and Tory, Conservative and Philistine, artistic and patriotic. This is due not merely to his fine cosmopolitanism, elevated above any Florentine idea of *fuori*, but to the obvious advantages afforded by such situations for the trial and purgation of character Emergencies and exigencies like these provide ample and easy material for the Comic Spirit alert to understand the workings of our British nature. Too busy to be diverted by the contemporary revival of mediævalism, Meredith has strenuously warred against the solid materialism and complacent impervious-

Introduction

ness to ideas which, in his judgment, distinguish and imperil the fat, opulent epoch lying under his own eyes. How ironical is such a use of the English novel! In Meredith's hands it is a sort of boomerang, as is apparent when we recollect the circumstances of its origin, in an essentially unheroic and prosaic society of people, who were (as T. H. Green excellently puts it) quite "self-satisfied and pleased with their surroundings." Satire lavished on this state of things is not effective. Native obtuseness proves too thick for most of its quick shafts. Besides, properly speaking, the satirist is but semi-artistic; like the bluebottle, to borrow from Emilia's fancy, he only sings when he is bothered. Meredith has the gentler and more piercing method of delicately analysing a decadent society to itself, and assisting health by the revelation of innate capacities for mischief as subtle and formidable as bacilli. An artist to the finger-tips, he would be inadequately described as a man of letters. He is that, but he is more. Not unlike Hugo and Tolstoy, he can allow his art to be saturated with his ethic, and yet retain the essentials of

George Meredith

the artist's glamour; which is wise indeed
for an author who addresses people rightly
suspicious of prose or verse that has designs
upon them. But this ethical interest steers
wide of malignant irony and cynicism, those
barbarian forms of humour. They are spiteful
and superior. They represent a savage type
of the genuine Comic Spirit, and Meredith is
at pains to show, in characters like Adrian
Harley and Colney Durance, how ineffective and subordinate a place is assigned to
the satirical temper in the direction of
affairs. What are the spurts of satire?
"Darkening jests on a river of slime." The
Comic Spirit is a spirit of silvery laughter.
"You may estimate your capacity for comic
perception by being able to detect the
ridicule of them you love, without loving
them less." Meredith's art, indeed, like that
of all genuine humourists, rises from deep
pools of gravity. Laughter, with him, to be
legitimate must be the child of sympathy and
of delight. It is infinitely serious, too serious
to be cynical or pessimistic. To be cynical,
he bluntly declares, is merely the raw
attempt of the worldly man to appear deep;

Introduction

as a form of mental and moral superficiality, it should be dismissed by the penetrative observer with derision. Neither depression nor scepticism is the ultimate attitude towards the inconsistencies and errors of the race. "Who is the coward among us? He who sneers at the failings of Humanity." "What is contempt," he asks again, "but an excuse to be idly minded, or personally lofty, or comfortably narrow, not perfectly humane?" Meredith never sneers. He is never savage or morose, hardly ever mocking in the vein of Ibsen and Anatole France, though he can be caustic when he chooses. The controlling principle of his work is to be nobly serious and witty, often in the same breath. Wit with him has a surgical function in contemporary society, but this does not involve an accumulation of physiological details or the pursuit of human documents. Folly indeed seems to him capable of ever new shapes in an effeminate and decadent age. A pestilence flieth abroad ; but its infection is to be met by common-sense allied to laughter. "The vigilant Comic Spirit as the genius of thoughtful laughter"—

21

George Meredith

such is Meredith's contribution to the moral
sanitation of the day. It is too intellectual, too
limited in its range, too rarefied, to be a perfect purge, but it has a function of its own.
He is never done praising laughter, thoughtful laughter. It clears the heart, as thunder
clears the air. It is the wine and bread
of sanity. In his opinion, one great cure
for the age and its troubles would be
reached if people could be persuaded first of
all to laugh at themselves a little, and thus
get rid of silly pride and obstinacy; then to
laugh, with trembling in their mirth, at other
people, instead of growing impatient and
angry at the follies and affectations of the
race. Folly is the natural prey of the Comic
Spirit; and if people are to be lifted out of
folly, with its pretensions, its love of posing,
its indulgence of the senses or the emotions
at the expense of the mind, the first step is to
make them smart and meditate. Meredith,
like Thackeray, although with weapons of a
different calibre, strikes at his age, with its
absurdities and maladies, in a splendid discon-
tent. But his blows are as positive in direction as they are delivered with artistic grace.

Introduction

To resume a simile applied somewhere by Chateaubriand to Cromwell's revolutionary methods, he destroys what he encounters in much the same peremptory and deliberate fashion as Michael Angelo destroyed the marble with his chisel.

Unflinching realism of this kind helps to make Meredith's optimism both grateful and convincing. "I can hear a faint crow of the cocks of fresh mornings far, far, yet distinct." However the artistic merits of the two writers be adjusted, there is no doubt that the moral atmosphere in Thomas Hardy's novels is distinctly autumnal : in Meredith, upon the other hand, it is that of a bright, keen day in spring, when to be out-of-doors is a healthy joy for those who do not mind tingling ears and cheeks slapped by the rain. This—were the word less ugly— might be termed his meliorism. He stands much nearer to an invigorating cordial Scandinavian, like his contemporary Björnson, than to the sombre genius of Ibsen. He contests and challenges, because it seems to him worth while to do so. The tide is usually turning on his beach. Face all the facts, he

23

George Meredith

insists, instead of shrouding inconvenient things in a painted veil of sentiment; yet as eagerly he urges "the rapture of the forward view," and with elastic optimism hurries on to administer a sharp rebuke to those who nod gloomily and dolefully over progress, breaking into Jobisms over the nightmare of "life as a wheezy crone." Ideals, or idols, are not always gifted with two legs. What of that? "Who can really think and not think hopefully?" "When we despair or discolour things, it is our senses in revolt, and they have made the sovereign brain their drudge. . . *There is nothing the body suffers, that the soul may not profit by.* . . Philosophy bids us to see that we are not so pretty as rosepink, not so repulsive as dirty drab; and that the sight of ourselves is wholesome, bearable, fructifying, finally a delight." Here we have the ethical soul of Meredith articulate. It is an optimism which is surer of itself than in Matthew Arnold, and less exasperating, because drawn from deeper fountains, than in Browning; on its horizon there is the promise, absent from Mark Rutherford's quiet and gray skies, of

Introduction

a dawn with uplifting power. Meredith
knows his Richter, and many sections of his
philosophy are little more than a brilliant
expansion and application of the German's
adage: be great enough to despise the world,
and greater in order to esteem it. Only from
such a mental attitude does endurance flow:
> "A fortitude quiet as Earth's
> At the shedding of leaves."

Progress, accordingly, is bound up with
mental and moral discipline, alike for men
and nations. "Strength is not won by
miracle or rape." Shibli must be thwacked,
if he is to reach his goal, and the resolute
philosophy of thwacking—for mind no less
than for body and fortune—pervades all
Meredith's romances. It is the only way to
cure egoism with its arrogance and mischief.
> "Lo! of hundreds who aspire,
> Eighties perish—nineties tire!
> They who bear up, in spite of wrecks and
> wracks,
> Were seasoned by celestial hail of thwacks.
> Fortune in this mortal race
> Builds on thwackings for a base."

Or, as Dr. Middleton rudely shocked that
arch-sentimentalist Sir Willoughby Patterne

by blurting out, all unwhipped boys make ill-balanced men. "They won't take rough and smooth as they come. They make bad blood, can't forgive, sniff right and left for approbation, and are excited to anger if an east wind does not flatter them. . . We English beat the world, because we take a licking well." The rain and wind blow through Meredith's verse and prose, and they form by no means an accidental setting. He is an obstinate believer in the sweet uses of adversity, and spends pages of instruction and amusement in an effort to commend the old thesis that the bloom of health comes to the soul as to the body by frank battling with the elements, not by luxurious coddling within doors. "I am well and 'plucky,' —a word which I propose to substitute for 'happy' as more truthful." In this remark of George Eliot to Mrs. Bray there is a good deal of Meredith's philosophy about facing facts and accepting adversity bravely.

It is at this point that the Comic Spirit pounces, with relentless beak, upon the two cardinal foes to health and progress in contemporary life. These are both born of the

Introduction

habit of taking ourselves too seriously, and their names are pride and sentimentalism. To avoid thwackings, to neglect inconvenient ideas and experiences, to shelter oneself behind incredulity or disdain from awkward things in the rough, actual world, is the chosen paradise of quite a host of men and women. Meredith's soul does not weep in secret for this mischievous and widespread pride. He darts on it like an unhooded falcon. From first to last, with all his gaiety and gravity, he is engaged in exposing the pride of egoism, to its own shame and good. Social ambition— the disposition to rise in the world—naturally forms its most obvious expression, as in "The House on the Beach," or better still in that most pitiful tale "Rhoda Fleming" (more pitiful because wider than "The Tale of Chloe") and in the sparkling comedy of "Evan Harrington." But this had been for long exploited by Thackeray, and after all it forms a naive and therefore less dangerous symptom of the disease. "Dombey and Son," too, had lashed sufficiently the pride of mercantile position. Yet more subtle phases lie behind; the conceit of a peacock, as in the

George Meredith

strutting vanity of Shibli Bagarag ; a vain passion for hereditary distinction, as in "Harry
Richmond ;" an affectation of culture and re-
finement, as in the Misses Pole ; an attempt to
play Providence and cut down nature to suit
an artificial theory, as in Sir Austin Feverel:
and so on. Pride is a very Proteus in these
novels. You have the pride of injured feelings, the obstinate pride that (in Lord Ormont
and Lord Fleetwood, 'the base Indians' of
their tribe) inflicts cruelty half unwittingly
upon others and even starves itself for some
fancied insult; you have the pride, half
creditable, half Quixotic, that drives Richard
Feverel from his wife and child, in a passage
which Stevenson, with brave enthusiasm,
pronounced the "strongest since Shakespeare,
in the English tongue"; you have the feudal
pride of Egoism, a narrow self-confidence
which calmly appropriates as much of the
world as it can reach and as calmly dooms the
rest. In short, if "passions spin the plot,"
the master-passion with Meredith's heroes
and heroines is pride. Or rather, we should
say, false pride. For the author is quick
to allow that "a man's pride is the front and

Introduction

headpiece of his character, his soul's support
or snare." It is a snare in almost all the
Meredith-romances, to lover, husband, father,
man of the world. Life is continually netting
itself in the meshes of false pride ; in a
refusal to admit one has been wrong, in the
disinclination to repair a mistake, in the habit
of clinging at all costs to belief in one's own
superior wisdom, in the greed of admiration,
or the dislike of criticism. The battle of false
pride is always against itself, and Meredith is
never finer, he is seldom more satisfying, than
in portraying this struggle of the soul to ex-
tricate itself from the results of a past impulse
of passion or from the coil of inherited prejudice. Tragedy with him consists in showing
how this awakening is either inadequate or
too late, and failure (in the last analysis)
means pride imperfectly beaten out of life.
"Surely an unteachable spirit," he declares, "is
one of the most tragic things in life." Which
is a variation upon Carlyle's favourite thesis
that no one falls into misery without having
first tumbled into folly. Perhaps the irony of
this is even less evident in the sullen forms of
pride than in the disasters that await sheer,

George Meredith

irrepressible, good-natured souls like Roy Richmond and Victor Radnor, in whom false pride exists as a lovable but fatal spirit of sanguine and infatuated buoyancy.

To sentimentalism, or emotional self-indulgence, which forms the companion weed of highly civilized society, Meredith is equally remorseless. Here also there is to be detected, in his judgment, a fatal lack of that inward and thorough grappling with the facts of life (and by facts Meredith does not exclude ideas) which is the fundamental virtue of his ethic. The sentimentalist lives in unrealities. He looks at Nature with his eyes half-closed, or else he considers some select portions of her. Factitious and morbid, he is a dilettante playing delicately and selfishly with extracts from the Book of Life; the result being that his opinions and aims are essentially false, his aspirations generally little better than mere twitches of egoism, and his tenderness a petty whimper of false sympathy. Peace is his ideal, meaning a lotos-land of freedom from disturbance; "peace, that lullaby word for decay!" A character of this kind is the natural, trashy product of a fat soil, where

Introduction

wealth and leisure often can be adjusted so as
to shut off the elect from impolite Nature.
Sentimentalists, as Meredith goes on gravely
to explain, are a variety due to a long process
of comfortable feeding, but there is one difference between them and the pig. The pig
too passes through a training of rich nourishment. Only it is not in him combined with
an indigestion of high German romance.
Pray do justice to the pig! Particularly in
the "Egoist" and (with an unwonted note of
tragedy) in "Sandra Belloni," Meredith takes
wicked delight in analysing the absurdity and
mischief of a spirit which would varnish
civilization, or—in another metaphor—conceal the tails of those polished, stately creatures who inhabit culture's paradise. Carlyle
lashed this Werterism or Transcendentalism;
Heine mocked it; Emerson pricked it; Meredith laughed it out of court. Sentimentalism
in a word spells for him mental immaturity
and moral opium. It is, to use his own fine
aphorism, enjoyment without obligation, an
attempt to taste existence without incurring
responsibility. Upon the other hand, the
better policy of treating Nature frankly,

George Meredith

which Meredith shares with the scientific movement of the age, makes an incessant demand upon courage and brains, especially brains. If people are to peruse Nature with virile and keen intelligence—and by Nature Meredith seems to mean the whole system of accessible facts and forces within and around the human consciousness—an open eye and unflinching sincerity are required ; hence the earliest symptom of philosophy in man is aversion to sentimentalism, in the guise either of self-pity or Byronic melancholy or contempt for the world. Attempts to cheat Nature by ignoring the flesh, for example, are not much less mischievous than the tendency to idolize it. Asceticism and sensuality alike, he is careful to point out, rest upon a common basis of sentimentalism, which is fundamentally onesided and consequently vicious ; and no reader of "The Egoist" is likely to forget the merciless exposure of a pseudo-Puritanism which in aesthetic and aristocratic superiority bans the rough, wholesome world. Sex and the senses have their place somewhere in the moral order, and it is always a grateful service to have the truth enunciated

Introduction

afresh that Nature with her plain and bracing laws cannot be misjudged or undervalued by any man, however civilized, with impunity. That applies to enigmas as well as to aspirations. "We do not get to any heaven by renouncing the Mother we spring from; and when there is an eternal secret for us, it is best to believe that Earth knows, to keep near her, even in our utmost aspirations." Thus Meredith finds but empty flashes in the sham spiritualism, so characteristic of the early Victorian age, which affects in prudery or piety to obliterate the physical. To stigmatize it is senseless; to decorously conceal it is hypocrisy and in the long run—though sometimes the run is not very long—sheer cruelty. The natural precedes the spiritual, which invariably presupposes it. "Nature, though heathenish, reaches at her best to the footstool of the Highest. Through Nature only can we *ascend*. St. Simeon saw the Hog in Nature, and took Nature for the Hog." But if this uglier under-side of things has to be reckoned with in philosophy and practice, without dainty shudders, it is wholly misconceived by those who regard it callously.

33

George Meredith

There is no vulgar realism in Meredith. He stands remote from the voluptuousness of the early Swinburne and from the strange acquiescence in man's earthly bias which recurs, sadly or savagely, in Thomas Hardy. A strong Rabelaisian love of wine and prizefighting and the like, running even to the verge of grossness, pervades some of his pages; but you are seldom allowed out of hearing of his own adages that "the mistake of the world is to think happiness possible to the senses," and that "all life is a lesson that we live to enjoy but in the spirit." With this proviso, it may be fairly said that uncompromising reality is the supreme note of his ethic; a note echoed by the one poet of our own day who approaches Meredith upon this plane—I mean Mr. William Ernest Henley. Clough is as sincere in resenting the habit of playing tricks with the soul, but his sincerity is practically helpless. The sum of Meredith's deliverance is that you are stepping down not up, if you are amiably taking opium in the soul or singing lullabies to the brain, instead of resolutely facing the web of cause and consequence in their real, actual proportions.

Introduction

Failure to see this elementary principle, he attributes not inaccurately to cowardice, which is simply a form of mental blindness. And when conscience is only a passenger, with the passions and prejudices working the vessel, and the brain a prisoner in the state-cabin, the uncertainty of the future merely consists of the variety of ways in which the final disaster may arrive. "Resolution," we are told, "is a form of light, our native light in this dubious world." The worst charge against sentimentalism is that it festers a flabby, stupid character, in which courage, the courage of veracity, is melted away.

Thanks to their conventional training, at least in the earlier Victorian periods at which Meredith's novels began to appear, women especially are apt to find themselves from time to time in a trying situation, before or after marriage, where they are hampered or put in a somewhat false position. Meredith is never weary of depicting such phases of experience, in which moral courage is the one path to safety (not to say, honour), and yet often the least obvious or easy resource open to "those artificial creatures called women who dare not be spontaneous, and cannot act independently if they would continue to be admirable in the world's eye." They have to avoid motion, in order "to avoid shattering or tarnishing." That is perhaps why his heroines, like some of George Eliot's, annoy us by the marriages they make. Meredith's ideal is a clear-sighted, free, and sensible womanhood, and he has a rude contempt for the weak, clinging, girl and her emotional delights. The bevy of girls, mainly English, who constitute one of the most charming features in his fiction, are no "wandering vessels crying for a pilot," but healthy, open-eyed mates. What a splendid company they are! Besides Renée and Ottilia, you live with Diana Warwick, Cecilia Halkett, Jenny Denham, Clara Middleton ("the dainty rogue in porcelain"), Rose Jocelyn, Emilia, Aminta, Carinthia ("the haggard Venus"), Julia Rippenger, Elizabeth Ople, Nesta Radnor, Annette, and Jane Ilchester—

> A troop of maids, brown as burnt
>   heather-bells,
> And rich with life as moss-roots
>   breathe of earth,
> In the first plucking of them.

Introduction

For the womanhood of his women, in their passage from girlhood to maturity and in their relations with one another as well as with men, the highest praise that need be given to Meredith is that he makes us think, and think without incongruity, of Shakespeare. His heroines have both character and charm; they are fresh, bright creatures, with a native bloom upon them, and he is versatile enough to succeed with other types; e.g., the clever old ladies, headed by Lady Eglett and Lady Camper (in that little perfect tale of her relations with General Ople), or the stout, cheery, vulgar women represented by Mrs. Berry, Mrs. Crickeldon, and the inimitable Mrs. Chump, who rank with the nurse in "Romeo and Juliet." It is only another taste of his fine quality, in the reading of woman, which the reader finds in the mischievous etchings of the Countess de Saldar, or of Livia and Henrietta in "The Amazing Marriage," the Misses Pole—especially Cornelia—and the feminine pariahs in "Richard Feverel" and "One of Our Conquerors." *Per contra,* Meredith has a Brontesque antipathy to the "veiled, virginal dolly-heroine" of ordinary fiction, just as he shows little regard for those who fling over the traces of their sex to "trot upon the borders of the Epicene." Start women on that track, and it is a race-course ending in a precipice. His golden hope seems to be a witty, charming woman, of clear intellect and free movement, yielding not a feather of her womanliness for some portion of man's strength. If Beauchamp, we may guess, was his own favourite hero, Diana Warwick embodies most of the feminine qualities which he desiderates. The "Ballad of Fair Ladies in Revolt" is sufficient proof that he was in full sympathy with the modern reaction of woman against the conventional restraints of a position which was generally disposed to treat her as a sort of fringe upon human nature, or a creature bound to go in bit and blinkers. Nevertheless, respect for her is assumed as a test of social health. It is the civilization, not the abolition, of marriage which her best friends will advocate. Anything less, however specious, means a dance to dissolution. There are a dozen passages in Meredith which indicate this cardinal idea of his social ethics. Consistently upon the

Introduction

side of women in their demand for a fuller
scope, instead of being forced to "march and
think in step, the hard-drilled Prussians of
society," he is as resolutely against any wild,
crude claim for rights which would ignore the
individual quality of woman or obliterate the
natural distinctions of sex. He would probably have refused to join Ibsen in shaking
down the pillars of conventional society.
Samson is not his model in reform. His policy
rather is lustily to drive out the Philistines
from the temple. Naturally, "the ancient
game of two," which ends or at least develops
in marriage, can hardly fail to form a central problem for any writer who deals with
the bases of modern society ; and Meredith's
triumph is that upon this ground he has
created women who have brains and judgment, yet are women to the core. What are
the "Maid of Air" and the "Grace of Clay"
compared to the loveliness of the truly natural
woman filled with God's fire ? He is neither
for Lesbia nor for Beatrice, neither for
Aspasia nor for Hypatia ; his quarrel with
the average man on behalf of woman is that
she is wronged by having false demands made

39

of her, being usually expected to form some sort of accompaniment to a tune played by the lordly male. Vittoria's wit and courage, for example, are missed by Carlo Ammiani after marriage ; she is but "a little boat tied to a big ship," and even Nevil Beauchamp smiles at the idea of a pretty woman exercising her mind independently, much less moving him to examine his own. Meredith's indignant heart is surely in Diana Warwick's epigram, "Men may have rounded Seraglio Point ; they have not yet doubled Cape Turk." "What Nature originally decreed," he said once, "men are but beginning to see, namely, that women are fitted for most of the avenues open to energy, and by their entering upon active life they will no longer be open to the accusation men so frequently bring against them of being narrow and craven."

In their loves, enthusiasms, and appetites Meredith likens women somewhere to boys, and it would be tempting to enlarge on his boys—another of the conspicuous successes in his work, possibly because (when unspoiled) boys exhibit a nonchalant, fresh, unsentimental attitude to things in general. Fortunately,

Introduction

anyone who knows Meredith knows Heriot, Temple, little Collett, and Ripton, as he knows Sam Weller or the rustics in Thomas Hardy's novels. We must be content to take boys farther on in their career.

"The chief object in life, if happiness be the aim and the growing better than we are, is to teach men and women how to be one; for if they're not, then each is a morsel for the other to prey on." Absorbed in this dilemma of the sexes, Meredith concentrates his efforts, not only on man's treatment of woman, but on man's ideal of himself. One of his real contributions to social ethics is the analysis of the true gentleman, particularly in "Evan Harrington" and "Sandra Belloni." As an observer of English society, he has only derision for false gentility, an antipathy which, like the enthusiasm for prizefighting and gipsies, he shares with George Borrow. Upon the other hand, he evidently seeks to destroy the prevalent delusion that good nature is a form of weakness and "strength" to be measured by self-assertion. He is strong in heroes, but they are of an original type. The flamboyant, brilliant man seldom comes to

George Meredith

much in Meredith's romances. Self-confident,
young characters generally drop into disaster,
from Alvan to Victor Radnor, in a sense from
Nevil Beauchamp to Lord Fleetwood. The
quiet, strong, trustworthy nature, again, gets
a far larger stroke in Meredith than (for
example) in Thackeray. Major Dobbin and
Warrington win nothing like the reward that
falls to such men as Redworth, Merthyr
Powys, Dartrey Fenellan, Austin Wentworth,
Seymour Austin, Owain Wythan, Vernon
Whitford, and Matthew Weyburn. They lack
or at any rate are outshone in social arts and
graces, but they possess solid qualities that
manage somehow to bring them out successful in the end. Impetuousness and bubbling
ardour play the rocket's career in Meredith.
His avowed partiality is for the drab men—
"drab" being the antithesis of "effervescing"
and "irrepressible"—for men of deep, self-
controlled natures, who refuse lightly to kindle
at the spark of personal ambition, and who—
above all—will not stoop to regard women as
objects upon which to practise daintily the
fowler's art. Clean, brave, unselfish and intelligent are Meredith's high adjectives for man.

42

Introduction

These ideals of womanhood and manhood run up into Meredith's general conception of human nature as part of Nature. The latter conception is developed principally in his poetry, but it underlies his prose, and the novels cannot be intelligently read apart from some grasp of what he means by the Earth or Nature. It is not a mere accessory to human life and feeling, a background to be painted in, by way of contrast or harmony. Meredith's Nature is, as in Aristotle—to quote Professor Butcher's definition—, "not the outward world of created things; it is the creative force, the productive principle of the universe." Nature in these novels and poems is vital, radiant, and supreme, a living presence which reminds us of the pulsing, all-embracing Nature of Lucretius, and, in certain other aspects, of Nature as the expression and embodiment of that divine wisdom for man which Marcus Aurelius inculcated. The distinctive value of Meredith's teaching on this point, however, is that nature is for him deeper and more complex than it could be for the ancient stoics. His Nature is the cosmos of evolutionary science. "The Ordeal of Richard

George Meredith

Feverel," as we have seen, was published in the same year as "The Origin of Species," and the salient feature of Meredith's work is that it has been carried out in full view of the contemporary scientific movement which seeks in Nature the ethical standards as well as the physical origin of man. The cardinal principle of his ethical idealism is the trustworthiness of the moral instincts. Nature is a living organism, whose end for man is spiritual, not material, and human life is unintelligible apart from its relationship to natural facts and forces. Life according to Nature is man's destiny, which means, not the worship of the senses, nor the ascetic denial of the senses, but the spirit's control of the senses. The end of Nature is man's ethical completeness. Neither the mind, nor the senses, nor the soul, is to be starved, but each and all must play their part in the drama of being.

> "Blood and brain and spirit, three
> Join for true felicity.
> Are they parted, then expect
> Some one sailing will be wrecked."

The beginning of wisdom, therefore, is to

Introduction

let Nature reach and teach us; otherwise it is
not possible to perceive man's ideal or the
conditions under which it can be realised.
This requires courage, for self and the senses
render man disinclined to face and welcome
the total order of Nature.

> "The senses loving Earth or well or ill
> Ravel yet more the riddle of our lot.
> The mind is in their trammels."

Most forms of contemporary pessimism and
sentimentalism are traced by Meredith to this
handicap—the refusal to confront the order of
Nature frankly and fully.   Only the mind or
brain is equal to this task.   If a man dares
to face and trust Nature, he is rewarded with
hope and insight.   If he does not, his view of
the world and of himself is distorted.   Thus
—to take but one example—cynicism is bound
up with a false view of Nature.   "You hate
Nature," says Gower Woodseer to the cynical
Lord Fleetwood, "unless you have it served
on a dish by your own cook.   That's the way
to the madhouse or the monastery.   There we
expiate the sin of sins. A man finds the
woman of all women fitted to stick him in the
soil, and trim and point him to grow, and

George Meredith

she's an animal for her pains! The secret of your malady is, you've not yet, though you're on the healthy leap for the practices of Nature, hopped to the primary conception of what Nature means. Women are in and of Nature." False views of oneself, as well as of the other sex, whether these views are ascetic or sensual, proceed from the same root, according to Meredith. A primary conception of Nature is a-wanting.

This primary conception involves not only a just relation of the sexes but their common interest in self-sacrifice, brotherliness, and unselfishness. Nature's supreme function is to recall her children from their moods of indulgence and egotism to the higher discipline of helpfulness. The great thing to think about, Meredith reiterates, is not reaping but sowing (compare, *e.g.*, the fifth chapter of "Lord Ormont and his Aminta," and "Vittoria" throughout). His passionate recoil from anything like luxurious individualism, and his stress on human fellowship as the true sphere of Nature's revelation, spring from his reading of her primary law—the law of sacrifice and service. Nature's crown and flower is man,

Introduction

but man conscious that personality means
kinship and helpfulness to his fellows. As
the author puts it, in Vittoria's ringing stanza
at Milan:

> Our life is but a little holding, lent
> > To do a mighty labour; we are one
> With heaven and with the stars, when
> > > it is spent
> > To serve God's aim: else die we
> > > with the sun.

"Service," said Diana Warwick, "is our destiny in life and death. Then let it be my
choice, living to serve the living, and be fret-
ted uncomplainingly."

The joy of Earth belongs to those who thus
enter intelligently and bravely into the order
of her discipline, which aims at speeding the
race upwards to God and good. This is the
burden of Meredith's philosophy, and it lifts
him clear of any languid or defiant or suspicious attitude towards Nature. He has a
coherent, balanced view of human nature;
he believes that men are meant for good; and
he is sure that Nature or the universe is on
their side in the struggle against lust and passion. "I say the profoundest service that

poems or any other writings can do for their reader is not merely to satisfy the intellect, or supply something polished and interesting, nor even to depict great passions or persons or events, but to fill him with vigorous and clean manliness, religiousness, and give him *good heart* as a radical possession and habit." That sentence of Walt Whitman sums up the drift of Meredith's prose as well as of his verse. There is not a whimper in it, not an atom of cowardice. He invigorates the reader while he amuses. And he does so, claiming to present the right order and use of life, because he has read Earth deep enough to see the rose of the soul unfold itself bravely under the grey skies of evolutionary science. The novels testify to this conviction in grave, buoyant, and energetic prose. They are studies in several types of human character, tragic and comic, designed to expound the bracing philosophy of Nature as that is interpreted by the Spirit of Comedy (in the Meredithian sense of the term), which is "the fountain of sound sense, not the less perfectly sound on account of the sparkle."

Novels written in this vein cannot fail

Introduction

to have a keen interest and value of their own, but it is superfluous to observe that their appeal is to a circle which must be comparatively restricted. This subtle, intellectual treatment of human nature in prose fiction, through the medium of the "Comic Spirit," addresses itself to people of sharp perception and sensitive faculties, even when the subjects are by no means recondite in themselves. A writer like Meredith finds his audience as well as his material, not in the marketplace, but in a society of quick-witted, cultured beings. A certain nimbleness of mind is requisite for the appreciation of his work, and this implies, as he is well aware, that his audience constitutes "an acute and honourable minority." For the crowd prefers to be thumped rather than tickled, and resents fiction being ranked as an elect handmaiden to philosophy.

Thanks to his high conception of the English novel and its function, Meredith makes little or no attempt to catch the multitude with broad effects, high colours, or strong flavours. His work has an extra-ordinary range. But, like Diana Warwick,

D

he does not lay himself out as a writer for "clever transcripts of the dialogue of the day, and hairbreadth escapes," breathless adventures, gushing sentiment, and the ooze of pathos. Consequently the atmosphere is somewhat rarefied at times. Certainly it cannot be described as wholly congenial to the average Briton, an excellent person who commonly prefers blunt, hard satire, humour with its i's dotted and its t's carefully crossed. As Meredith himself confesses genially, "the national disposition is for hard-hitting with a moral purpose to sanction it"; ethereal, nimble wit does not allure the many. As handled by Meredith, it is often clear and true. But it invokes "the conscience residing in thoughtfulness," and comedy of this kind must frequently be content to play to empty benches. To the first edition of "Modern Love" he prefixed the lines:

"This is not meat
For little people or for fools."

Unfortunately it is apt to become food for a cult or coterie, which is a serious handicap upon any writer.

So far as an author's refusal to be simple is

Introduction

wilful and affected, the public revenges itself by visiting him with an unworthy but not undeserved neglect. Now, two spirits struggle for the soul of Meredith as a literary artist. There is a lyric, spontaneous feeling, which now and then issues in passages of direct intuition and unaffected charm, vibrating with emotion and pure fancy. Meredith has his "native woodnotes wild"; and they are by no means confined to his prose, as readers of poems like "Juggling Jerry" and "Love in a Valley" (especially in its original version) will gladly testify. Along with this, however, a spirit of strain and affectation makes itself heard. There is a tone of painful artifice in him, of which *e.g.* "Modern Love," the later odes, and "One of Our Conquerors" bear melancholy traces. Whole pages of Meredith's work are spoiled by a passion for the intricate. It is as though he were fascinated by anything off the high road: complex motives, tangled situations, abstruse points of conduct. "In Our fat England," he pleads unabashed, "the gardener Time is playing all sorts of delicate freaks in the hues and traceries of the flower of life, and shall we not note them? If we are to understand our species, and mark the progress of civilization at all, we must." To which one would be inclined to answer not by a simple negative but by drawing distinctions, and especially by demurring to the implication that twists and freaks are anything but a subordinate element in average human existence. To Meredith, in fact, the flower of life is an orchid oftener than a lily of the field. His predilection for subtle shades and traceries tends to present ordinary life to him as morally exotic. His creative imagination redeems him, certainly; the natural sights and sounds that fill his pages protect the reader generally against any prolonged sense of artificiality. I would not go nearly so far as to say that nothing seems to interest him strongly except "derangement, the imperceptible grain of sand that sets the whole mechanism out of gear." That is true, but it is not all the truth, although one can readily understand how a case for this verdict could be strongly and unfairly stated, if critics persist in remaining blind to the fact that the dramatic *motif* in a novel of Meredith is

Introduction

really never far-fetched. Its variations and developement, however, often are. "The light of every soul burns upward; let us allow for atmospheric disturbance." This would be an adequate defence, were it not that in expatiating upon the allowance and watchfully detecting the whirl of motes within the beam, he now and then seems clean to forget that he has a taper needing his attention.

The difficulty is aggravated by his fondness for developing a story by diverting allusions rather than by plain straightforward narrative. It is a vexatious and often an inartistic method. Meredith has usually a story to tell, and plenty of emotion and adventure wherewith to carry it forward. Only, you must go behind the booth and see the showman working his puppets. The result is that the characters are not always kept at blood-heat, while the impatient spectator's interest is first divided and then apt to flag. In reading some of the novels for the first time you feel like a small man in a crowd, when some procession is passing—bewildered and aggrieved. Colour and movement are there; but they are neither coherent nor made obvious to you. In a more poetical figure, the stream of narrative is so overlaid at some places with lilies of comment and aphorism, that the current is seriously impeded and the flow of water almost hidden. No doubt the lilies are fresh and splendid ; but that is hardly the point at issue. The novelist is conscious of his fault. He is constantly pausing, especially in the later novels, to apologise for the intrusion of the philosopher upon the artist and for the marriage of comedy and narrative, but his contrite excuses remind one too vividly of Falstaff's. The habit seems too strong for him. Partly it is a defect of his intense in-tellectualism ; partly it is one consequence of his analytic principle that the ideas rather than the appetites of men form the best clue to their conduct. But in any case he is open to severe criticism upon this point of technical execution. Like all mannerisms it has probably been aggravated by the partial obscurity in which the author had for long to work. Absence of popular recognition upon a scale commensurate to a man's ability is apt to foster any innate tendency to mental perversi-ties, just as the bodily gestures of a recluse

Introduction

acquire insensibly a certain uncouth awkwardness ; and Meredith is not wholly to be acquitted of the artistic crime of eccentricity. Isolation here also has intensified an inborn freakishness of manner. "Mystic wrynesses he chased." No one would insist upon a novel of the highest rank furnishing the precise details of a reporting column; yet how few of Meredith's romances would have been spoiled by the omission of some disquisitions upon mental pathology, and by the introduction of a little plain information about what exactly has been and is being done ! Is it only the "happy bubbling fool" who desires to know the progress as well as the causes of events ? In "Diana of the Crossways," for example (as in the "Amazing Marriage"), the opening chapter is devoted to a delightful preliminary talk, full of clever hints, anticipations, side allusions and the like, which certainly create an interest and atmosphere for the subsequent tale. But it is only in Chapter II. that the story plunges from exposition of feelings and gossip into the gay whirl of an Irish ball. "Let us to our story," says the author coolly, "the froth being out of the bottle." But surely the froth should be out of the bottle before it is held to the lips!

Admittedly the novelist is never feverish or fragmentary in manner, never a wayward visionary even in his exalted moments, never prolix or laborious in the sense in which George Eliot occasionally plays the pedant, almost never ornate or irrelevant like Balzac with his descriptions of locality and furniture. But as a composer he has a dangerous endowment of fertility, and one would rather that his affinities had been with any school except the German, from which—headed by Jean Paul Richter—it is not inapposite to conjecture that he has caught an inartistic forgetfulness of the boundaries that separate the essay and the romance. One is glad to have Hazlitt's countenance in finding the similar passages in Meredith's prototype, Molière, somewhat verbose and intricate; they are that, even when in the one case they are carried off by the rapid dialogue in verse, in the other by the flashing prose. At the worst they are never opaque or muddy—which is always something. But the trouble about these diverting and ingenious

Introduction

asides is that Meredith knows better.   If he likes, and fortunately he often likes, he can give his readers Stevenson's luxury of laying aside the judgment and being submerged by the tale as by a billow. The pity of it is that he prefers now and again to keep your head prosaically safe above the water, while he expounds to you in witty words the sequence of the tides.

A passion for the bizarre in action or character, accompanied by a preoccupation with the integral calculus of motives, is not unfitly set in a compressed form of utterance which is rich to the point of obscurity. Meredith's style reflects his mental temper of keen, pregnant observation.   It is terse and quick and brilliant; but it has a tendency, where inspiration flags, to lapse now and then into euphuism, extravagance, oversubtlety.   It has oftener the flashing edge of crystals than limpid fluidity.   Language becomes with him in certain moods a shower of audacious and prismatic epigrams, or "a flushed Bacchanal in a ring of dancing similes."   There is little or none of Swinburne's riot in verbiage, or of Ruskin's

billowy rhetoric. The writer seems nervously
and even awkwardly to avoid all approaches
to smooth and flexible expression. The style is
difficult, but through sheer excess of thought,
not through confusion. It is never plush,
though too frequently it becomes brocade,
rather than the silk which closely fits the
limbs. Stiff in parts, though jewelled, it is
apt to hang in somewhat rigid folds. There are
passages of his poetry, for example, compared
to which Sordello and Pacchiarotto are transcripts of lucidity.

Some of the common clamour about Meredith's style, however, is due to intellectual
torpidity. Years ago Mark Pattison observed
that Meredith's name was "a label warning
'novel readers' not to touch. They know
that in the volumes which carry that mark
they will not find the comfortable conventionalities and the paste diamonds which make
up their ideal of life. Worse than this,
Mr. Meredith's style requires attention; an
impertinent requirement on the part of a
novelist." Some people also fail to observe
that in the dialogues, for example, he is true
to life. Ordinary conversation as a rule

answers thoughts as well as words; it runs
on a level where the speakers address what
is meant rather than what is said. (Readers
of "Rhoda Fleming" will recollect a famous
instance.) Further, one is very seldom
annoyed in Meredith with quips and verbal
puzzles or with disagreeable attempts to paint
in words, and although the staccato movement
is somewhat clicking, it is never obtrusive in
his readings of Nature or in his love-scenes.
There one has not to pause and unravel a
paragraph or disentangle sense from a sentence. The clotted manner drops away,
confusion and inversion disappear, and the
result is a vivid transcript of reality. For
Meredith is like the historian, Green, "a jolly
vivid man . . . as vivid as lightning," to quote
Tennyson's verdict on the latter. In repro-
ducing subtle shades of feeling or in describing
physical impressions, he has a marvellous
skill; a handful of words becomes almost
transparent with imagination and delicate insight. No doubt, of his verse in large sections,
though seldom of his finer prose, it is not
extravagant to say that "the aim to astonish
is greater than the desire to charm."

George Meredith

"Forcible" suits him better than "urbane";
"dazzling," as a rule, better than "chaste"
or "Attic." A style naturally luminous and
picturesque sails perilously near the coasts
of tortuous euphuism; for by a strange
perversity he seems upon occasion to
court the very foppery of genius, till one
is sadly tempted to recall the tribe of
Donne and Cowley with their quaint and
cumbersome conceits. Sir Lukin sends a boy
to run for news of the score at a cricket-match
—"and his emissary taught lightning a lesson." That is Meredith all over, though his
"euphuism" is adventitious rather than essentially frigid and trivial. Yet, judged by
his best, and his best is the greater part of his
output, he has command of a diction almost
unrivalled for its purposes, surging and full
and radiant. It is a pure joy to read many of
his pages, were it only for their unflagging wit
and marvellous use of metaphor—that literary
gift which Aristotle singled out as a sure mark
of literary genius. Such qualities of style are
the reflection of mental splendour in any
writer, and, though cultivated, are never a
mere trick. Limpid simplicity indeed is not

Introduction

one of his main notes; which is to be regretted, as simplicity is one condition of vitality in literature. He tends to be elliptic and—in a good sense—embroidered, in language. In musical phrase there is more harmony and orchestration than melody in parts of his work; he is, perhaps, the Berlioz of modern prose-fiction in this country. But he has melody as well as counterpoint. The supreme qualities of brilliant phrasing, terseness of expression, energy, exquisite colouring, and luxuriant fancy, are all conspicuous in his style; they rightly count for much, and their wealth covers a great multitude of minor sins. If here and there he deserves the charge implied in Falstaff's retort to Pistol, one must remember that, judged by this standard, Shakespeare himself falls to be criticised like Meredith for the same offence. In both it is as patent as it is—comparatively speaking—venial. Shakespeare is king of the continent where Meredith is a prince; and Johnson's famous verdict on the Elizabethan recurs to the mind with curious persistency as one attempts to estimate the Victorian. "A quibble was to him the fatal Cleopatra for which he lost the world, and

was content to lose it. . . . I cannot say he is
everywhere alike. He is many times flat and
insipid. But he is always great when some
great occasion is presented to him ; no man
can say he ever had a fit subject for his art
and did not then raise himself as high above
his fellows, *quantum lenta solent inter viburna
cupressi.*"

This slight summary of some cardinal ideas
in Meredith's fiction, and of some salient
features in his technical method, will serve
perhaps to put one *en route* with him. I have
left myself no space to touch upon some other
fascinating aspects, such as his cosmopolitan
outlook, from which all insularity is purged :
his minor characters: his versatile humour :
his technical execution: his poetical workmanship: his relation to men like Dickens,
Balzac, Hugo, and especially Thomas
Hardy: his attitude to politics and progress:
his estimates of religion (in semitones,
scanty but firm), patriotism, education, and
the Celtic temperament. These and other
lines of study can be worked out from the
general standpoint which I have tried to suggest in this paper. For the primary thing to

Introduction

be insisted on with regard to Meredith is that in focussing his position we may with advantage look at the content rather than the form of his work. It is only consonant with his own avowed desire that we should thus approach him from the side of ethics as well as of art, although no huger injustice could be done to him than to claim him for a cult or for a party, much less to convey the impression that his novels are a species—even a glorified species—of pamphlets. Meredith is a master of literature. Some of his novels are triumphs of creative prose, and—despite their dependence upon a knowledge of contemporary feeling in nineteenth-century England—they will rank with the supreme contributions of last century to English literature, even although they win him security rather than fulness of fame. In style and conception, we may surely say, without being Meredithyrambic, that he is a peer of the few great literary artists in our age. His line and colour belong to the great style in literature, and three-fifths of his work is bathed in what his friend Swinburne called "passionate and various beauty." The artistic impulse asserts

George Meredith

itself in almost every chapter he has written, for in spite of the writer's rich mental constitution, his complexity of material is rarely suffered to compromise the symmetry and the movement which are essential to greatness in a genuine prose romance. Still, any eulogy of Meredith's intellectual subtlety and imaginative reach—and an estimate here passes quickly into eulogy—must be balanced by the admission that prose-fiction in his hands moves out into the strenuous and stirring tideway of contemporary life; he is highly serious for all his wit and charm, and he has not the slightest notion of enticing you into a house boat or a racing gig.

Some of you will remember this prose-parable by Maarten Maartens: "There was a man once—a satirist. In the natural course of time his friends slew him and he died. And the people came and stood about his corpse. 'He treated the whole round world as his football,' they said indignantly, 'and he kicked it.' The dead man opened one eye. 'But always toward the goal,' he said." Meredith is no satirist. He does not even turn a superb and deliberate censor of the universe

Introduction

like William Morris and John Ruskin;
though his aim is to waken and to brace his
age, he never ostentatiously lifts the scourge
or broom, and "kicking" is altogether too
coarse and direct an expression to denote his
genial influence.   But he is really aggressive,
in one sense.   He produces a distinct impact
upon "that conscience residing in thoughtfulness," which it is his design to exercise
and to increase.   Resent it or not as you
please, what Meredith is concerned with
is that you shall treat the novel as something
other than a brassy or a bun.   To stir the mind's
interest by a vital and varied application of
"the Comic Spirit," is the motive of George
Meredith.   He would make his prose both
voice and force.   If readers fling down his
works without being pushed an inch or two
nearer sanity and sincerity, or without sus-
pecting that these are a goal, or even without
dreaming that for them a goal exists at all,
then a fault lies somewhere.   But the fault
is not wholly Meredith's.

E

THE SHAVING OF SHAGPAT

The Shaving of Shagpat

"THE Shaving of Shagpat: An Arabian Entertainment," Meredith's first work in prose, was published in 1856, five years after his first book of poems. Beckford's "Vathek," which had appeared nearly seventy years earlier, "remained without distinguished progeny," says Professor Raleigh. But "Shagpat" is its late-born child. It also draws upon "The Arabian Nights," though Meredith easily outstrips Beckford in the skill by which he has caught the discursiveness, the luxuriant fancy, the riot of imagination, and the brilliant atmosphere of the Oriental phantasmagoria. Both novels are written in high spirits. But "The Shaving of Shagpat" is composed in a characteristic vein of the mock-heroic, with touches of passion and romance and exuberant humour. George Eliot, in one of her reviews, hailed it "as an apple tree among

69

George Meredith

the trees of the wood," and, once the public grew accustomed to its puzzling qualities, the wit and genius of this *tour de force* prevailed with its audience, although a second edition was not called for until 1865.

Three separate stories, "The Story of Bhanavar the Beautiful," "The Punishment of Shahpesh, the Persian, or Khipil the Builder," and "The Case of Rumdrum, A Reader of Planets, that was a Barber," are woven, in oriental manner, into the plot. But the outline of the main story is as follows :—

Noorna bin Noorka, a waif beside her dead mother in the desert, is rescued and reared by a certain chief Raveloke in the city of Oolb, where in her twelfth year she obtains from an old beggar—in return for a piece of gold given in charity—her heart's desire in dresses, gems, and toys, but especially a red book of magic. She becomes proficient in spells and sorcery, owing to her eagerness to discover her father, and thereby incurs the jealousy of Princess Goorelka, an accomplished sorceress, whose genie Karaz eventually manages to carry off

The Shaving of Shagpat

Noorna as his prize. She promises to give
herself to the possessor of the Identical, or
hair of fortune, which was on his head, in
return for his help in disenchanting her
father. The latter, Feshnavat by name, is
shown by Karaz to be one of a number of
birds in the aviary of Goorelka. These birds
are her former lovers, and they can only be
disenchanted if they are kept laughing for
one hour uninterruptedly. Noorna happens
by accident to gain possession of Goorelka's
magic ring which made its possessor "mistress of the marvellous hair which is a
magnet to the homage of men, so that they
crowd and crush and hunger to adore it,
even the Identical." She disenchants her
father, and then, anxious to evade her
promise to Karaz, discovers that, while the
hair Identical must live on some head, the ring
is powerless over it except in the genie's
head. She therefore manages to outwit
Karaz, tears the hair from his head, and
drops it on that of an innocent clothier called
Shagpat. Karaz forthwith becomes her rebellious slave. But he has his revenge. For
Goorelka had persuaded Noorna, who loved

flowers, to tend the Lily of Light upon
the Enchanted Sea, which meant that her
beauty was bound up with that of the Lily.
"Whatever was a stain to one withered the
other." Goorelka then blighted the petals
of the Lily and turned Noorna into a
wrinkled crone, ugly and tottering. Nevertheless Noorna, by the power of the ring,
is able to advance Feshnavat to the position
of vizier, and in the meantime she anxiously
awaits the coming of the barber who, as her
spells inform her, is destined to shave the
Identical from the head of the vain-glorious
Shagpat. For the worthy clothier, finding
himself the object of homage on account of
his hair, naturally remains unshorn, "a
miracle of hairiness, black with hair as he
had been muzzled by it, and his head as it
were a berry in a huge bush by reason of it."
The whole city, including the king, lies
under the enchantment of the hair. Only
Feshnavat and Noorna retain their wits,
and Shagpat audaciously claims the latter in
marriage.

It is at this juncture that the story opens.
Noorna's magic has revealed to her that

The Shaving of Shagpat

Shagpat is to be shaved by a certain youth who comes along a magic line which she draws from the sandhills outside the city. This youth is Shibli Bagarag of Shiraz, "nephew to the renowned Baba Mustapha, chief barber to the Court of Persia." Hungry and abject, Shibli is met by Noorna in her hag-like form, who persuades him that his fortune is made if he only succeeds in shaving Shagpat. The youth is vain and enterprising. He makes the attempt, and is soundly thwacked for the insult to Shagpat and the citizens; the latter indignantly throw him out of the city. Noorna however consoles him with the promise of honour and happiness, if he agrees to marry her. This, after some hesitation, he agrees to do. They are betrothed in the house of Feshnavat; Shibli is amazed to find that each of his rather reluctant kisses makes the hag become younger and prettier, whereupon Noorna reveals to his astonished ears the destiny to which he is appointed. The news turns his head. Noorna had already detected his conceit. "'Tis clear," she said to her father, "that vanity will trip him, but honesty is a

strong upholder." Shibli verifies this prog-
nostication by his swelling pride at the news
of what he was designed to accomplish. "He
exulted, and his mind strutted through the
future of his days, and down the ladder of
all time, exacting homage from men, his
brethren ; and 'twas beyond the art of Noorna
to fix him to the present duties of the enterprise : he was as feathered seed before the
breath of vanity."

The serious campaign now begins. Three
motives are at work in Shibli : the desire of
taking vengeance for the thwacking he had
received, the ambition excited by his destiny,
and a genuine love for Noorna. But the
obstacles are formidable. The first consists
of the illusions with which Rabesqurat, the
queen of the Enchanted Sea, has surrounded
Shagpat ; these "make it difficult to know
him from his semblances, whenever real
danger threateneth him." Secondly, there
is the weakness of natural man, who is un-
likely to finish off Shagpat at one effort.
And thirdly, there is the difficulty of getting
Shagpat ready for shaving, as well as the
trouble of finding a blade keen enough to

reap the magic hair which defies all mortal
razors. The only blade is a sword which is
to be found in Aklis, and to gain it three
charms are requisite. The first is (i) a phial
of water from the fountain of Paravid, each
drop of which makes flowers and stones and
sand to speak ; this, with the aid of Karaz,
Noorna enables Shibli to secure. (ii) Then
some hairs from the tail of the horse
Garaveen are required. But Shibli's incur-
able vanity prompts him to ride the dangerous steed, until, to save him, Noorna is
obliged to let Karaz seize Garaveen. She
manages to pull three hairs from the horse's
tail, but Karaz is now their foe, instead of
their slave, and Shibli has to return dolefully
to the city of Oolb, by aid of drops from his
magic phial. Noorna, in the form of a hawk,
rescues him *en route* from various perils,
enables him to shave the king and court of
Oolb, to steal the cockle-shell from under
the pillow of Goorelka, and, hotly pursued
by the latter, to tear up the Lily on the
Enchanted Sea, thus rescuing Noorna from
the spell of ugliness, and turning Goorelka
into a repulsive hag who is carried off by

Karaz. The Lily is the third help (iii) in their enterprise. Equipped with it, Noorna and Shibli make for the fairy mountain of Aklis. But first they must pass through the palace of Illusions, where Rabesqurat reigns as queen. Left to himself, Shibli succumbs to her Circe-like wiles, but manages to recover himself and to plunge on through similar seductions of vanity and ambition in the palace of Aklis. By the help of the seven sons of Aklis and their sister, Princess Gulrevaz, he secures the coveted Sword, at the price of all his three enchantments. His first task is to rescue poor Noorna who, by the spells of Rabesqurat, had been chained to a pillar in the sea ; this, however, is effected by Princess Gulrevaz and her magic bird Koorookh. Shibli now leaves Aklis with his precious sword, but unluckily he brandishes it with a silly flourish, in order to look through the veil that shrouded Rabesqurat as she ferried him across the sea to Noorna. The only cure for the disastrous illusions produced by this vision is to sleep in the bosom of his beloved ; thanks to the hair of Garaveen and to Abarak, Rabesqurat's

The Shaving of Shagpat

dwarf slave, he gets clear from Aklis and is rescued by Noorna, in whose lap he finds new manhood. Meantime Koorookh bears them safe into the desert, where Feshnavat joins them with the news that during their absence Shibli's uncle, the loquacious and irrepressible barber Mustapha, had been thwacked for daring to practise his craft in Oolb, and that in a subsequent fit of delirium he had—by the wiles of Goorelka disguised as a hag—contrived to ruin his protector Feshnavat. All this had contributed to the greater glory of Shagpat, who was at the zenith of his arrogance.

Feshnavat and his daughter now return to Oolb to mature the final plot. A fresh attempt by Mustapha, who gets the length of lathering Shagpat, is frustrated by Karaz in the form of a flea. By way of punishment the barber is condemned to try and shave Shagpat before the court ; at the third essay he is hurled ignominiously "like a stone from a sling, even into the outer air and beyond the city walls." The Identical blazes up for three days and three nights in triumph on the head of Shagpat who lies in a trance. But the

George Meredith

clothier's triumph is short-lived. On the
fourth day, after a fierce conflict of genii, the
flashing blade in Shibli's hand shaves Shagpat
clean, to the consternation of the populace ;
the Identical is shorn off, and "day was on
the baldness of Shagpat." So the story ends.
Baba Mustapha is hailed king of Oolb, and
Shibli marries Noorna.

The book is studded with scraps of verse and
aphorisms, some of which illustrate germi-
native ideas in the author's subsequent work.
Thus the power of Illusion is represented as
operating upon people of one idea. Queen
Rabesqurat is "the mistress of the single-
thoughted, and them that follow one idea to
the exclusion of a second." See below under
"Beauchamp's Career" and "One of Our
Conquerors." Shibli illustrates the mischief
done by airy conceit and also the profit of
chastening—both characteristic ideas of
Meredith's ethic. The former, as a source of
aberration, comes out also in the character of
Shagpat, lolling gravely in his shop before the
crowds who assembled to gaze at his shaggy
pate. Noorna exhibits the union of wit and
charm in a woman which Meredith is never

weary of commending, and the story closes by hinting that Shibli, unlike some other heroes of the later novels, respected the wisdom of his bride, while he admired her beauty. As for minor details, note that the love scene in "The Story of Bhanavar" is placed beside running water, as is so often the case in Meredith's romances, and that the power of laughing at oneself is pronounced the cure for pedantry and conceit. In the palace of Rabesqurat Shibli sees "divers sitters on thrones, with the diadem of asses' ears stiffened upright, and monkey's skulls grinning with gems; they having on each countenance the look of sovereigns and the serenity of high estate." As Shibli reflected, "if these sitters could but laugh at themselves, there would be a release for them, and the crown would topple off which getteth the homage of asses and monkeys."

The snatches of verse, which enliven "Shagpat" as well as "Farina," partly recall the quality of Meredith's early poems. When the latter were published, Dr. Hort wrote of them : "They are not deep, but show a rare eye and ear. There is a Keatsian sensuous-

George Meredith

ness about them, but the activity and *go* prevent it from being enervating and immoral." " I send a scrap of Meredith . . . is it not sweet and perfect in itself as a song ? Talk of Horace and Herrick ! It seems to me more like Shakespeare's songs." This enthusiastic criticism is borne out by several of the lyric stanzas in "The Shaving of Shagpat."

The story has been beset by misconceptions. Meredith anticipated one of them in a prefatory note to the first edition, which gravely explained that the work was not a translation. Another view of it has been more persistent. Attempts have been made to read an allegorical significance into the adventures of Shibli, as though that worthy person represented the true reformer who seeks to emancipate men from the old customs and abuses to which they bow down. Some ground for this theory might plausibly be found in the conclusion, where Meredith observes gravely that " the mastery of an Event lasteth among men for the space of one cycle of years, and after that a fresh Illusion springeth to befool mankind. As the poet declareth in his scorn :

The Shaving of Shagpat

'Some doubt Eternity : from life begun,
   Has folly ceased within them, sire to son ?
   So, ever fresh Illusions will arise
   And lord creation until men are wise.'"

But it is as vain to allegorise this story as
"Don Quixote." At the most, "The Shaving
of Shagpat," like "The Idylls of the King,"
has "an allegory in the distance"; no elaborate symbolism can be read into the details
of the plot. In fact, as early as the second
edition, Meredith humorously disclaimed
such an intention in another prefatory note.
"It has been suggested to me," he wrote,
"by one who has no fear of allegories on
the banks of the Nile, that the hairy Shagpat
must stand to mean umbrageous Humbug
conquering the sons of men; and that
Noorna bin Noorka represents the Seasons,
which help us, if there is health in us, to
dispel the affliction of his shadow; while
my heroic Shibli Bagarag is actually to be
taken for Circumstance, which works under
their changeful guidance towards our ultimate
release from bondage, but with a disappointing apparent waywardness. The excuse for

George Meredith

such behaviour as this youth exhibits, is so good that I would willingly let him wear the grand mask hereby offered to him. But, though his backslidings cry loudly for some sheltering plea, or garb of dignity, and though a story-teller should be flattered to have it supposed that anything very distinct was intended by him, the Allegory must be rejected altogether. The subtle Arab who conceived Shagpat, meant either very much more, or he meant less ; and my belief is, that, designing in his wisdom simply to amuse, he attempted to give a larger embrace to time than is possible to the profound dispenser of Allegories, which are mortal ; which, to be of any value, must be perfectly clear, and, when perfectly clear, are as little attractive as Mrs. Malaprop's reptile."

FARINA

Farina

"FARINA: A Legend of Cologne" was published in 1857. Slighter than "The Shaving of Shagpat," it is also a burlesque, although the subject is mediæval, not oriental. The story is a subtly ironical sketch of superstition and chivalry, which reminds one of Peacock's "Maid Marian" —itself a gentle satire on the romantic movement represented by M. G. Lewis and Sir Walter Scott. "Farina," however, with its blend of the supernatural and the heroic lies nearer to "The Abbot" and "The Monastery." At the close of the first chapter of "The Tale of Chloe," Meredith afterwards wrote that "A living native duke is worth fifty Phoebus Apollos to Englishmen, and a buxom young lass of the fields mounting from a pair of pails to the estate of duchess, a more romantic object than troops of your visionary Yseults and Guineveres." "Farina"

George Meredith

is a practical illustration of this scorn for the revival of mediævalism. In spite of its love-passages and fits of spirited narrative, it is hardly an adequate example of the writer's power over the short story, but it reflects his German education and one or two of his characteristic ideas.

Gottlieb von Groschen, a rich merchant and money-lender of Cologne, has one lovely daughter Margarita, in whose honour the youths of the city have formed a White Rose Club sworn to uphold her beauty against all comers. Only one youth, the slender, fair Farina, refuses to join this league of tender and quarrelsome fanatics. Farina is poor; as a student of chemistry, he is also suspected of tampering with the black art; but Margarita's heart is tender towards him, and he is in love with her.

The story opens three days before the entry of Kaiser Heinrichs into Cologne after a campaign on the Danube. A troop of wild cavalry, belonging to the robber baron Werner, of Werner's Eck, an independent royal adherent, ride into the city and attempt to offer an indignity to Margarita in front of

Farina

her father's house. Thanks to the intervention of a sturdy stranger, Guy the Gosshawk,
who is in the Kaiser's service, the girl is
rescued ; Werner rides up to scatter his un-
ruly followers ; and the Gosshawk is fêted by
the grateful Gottlieb, while Farina goes off,
rewarded for his share in the rescue by soft
words from Margarita's lips and a silver
arrow from her hair. Later in the evening,
Guy and he foregather, and, after some
nocturnal adventures in foiling an attack of
Schmidt, Werner's dupe and confederate,
upon Gottlieb's house, both are captured by
the White Rose Club who suspect them of
designs upon Margarita. Guy is released at
Gottlieb's request, but Farina, who has lost
his silver arrow during the night, is consigned
to prison.

Next day the prowling Werner sends a
forged letter from Farina to Margarita with
the silver arrow which Schmidt had picked
up. The note, however, is opened by the
girl's aunt Lisbeth, a sour and suspicious
prude, who thinks it best to keep the assig-
nation herself, in the disguise of her niece.
The result is that she is carried off to the

robber baron's castle. On discovering their mistake, the troopers return and secure Margarita who, after opening a letter to Lisbeth from her crony, Farina's mother, had gone to visit Farina in prison.

The plot is now complicated rather awkwardly by a combat on the Drachenfels between Satan and a mysterious monk who carries off Farina from prison to witness the ghostly combat. Meredith describes the latter in Lucianic style. Satan is openly vanquished and takes refuge underground in Cologne. Monk Gregory, inflated with a victory which is apparently complete, finds himself a spiritual hero ; but, instead of having Farina to corroborate his tale of prowess, he is deserted by that youth, who is off with Guy to rescue Margarita. The rescue is effected after a hand-to-hand conflict between Guy and the Baron, assisted by the supernatural agency of a Water-Lady who helps Farina into the castle and paralyses the Baron by announcing that his doom has come, inasmuch as a true lover (*i.e.*, Farina) has dipped three times in the stream round the Eck.

Returning to Cologne, the party meet the

Farina

White Rose Club, and, on discovering that
Lisbeth is still a prisoner in the castle, retrace
their steps to deliver her. Farina alone
proceeds to the city to resume his captivity
and take his place again beside monk Gregory.
The poor monk's hour of triumph has
passed into degradation. Satan's overpowering
stench, as he went underground, keeps the
Kaiser at a distance from the city, and the
blame of this pestilential odour is naturally
laid by the citizens upon the luckless ecclesi-
astic. Farina, however, solves the problem
and mends his own fortunes by furnishing
the Kaiser with a bottle of his new essence,
Eau de Cologne. The king and his army thus
find it possible to enter the city, and Farina's
reward is the hand of Margarita.

The main indications of promise in this
slight tale are Meredith's treatment of young
love, his description of the nightingales overheard by Farina outside the castle, and his
mastery of the art of being grave and absurd
in the same breath. Margarita is the first
sketch of later heroines like Jane Ilchester
and Aminta and Rose Jocelyn, with her
frank, blue eyes, and her mixture of boyish

George Meredith

camaraderie and womanly charm. Again, as in
"The Shaving of Shagpat," pride has its rôle ;
the monk Gregory boasts of his victory over
Satan, but has to confess : " How great must
be the virtues of them that encounter Sathanas!
Valour availeth naught. But if virtue be not
in ye, soon will ye be puffed to bursting with
that devil's poison, self-incense." It is noticeable, too, that while the ascetic, who has
forsworn the joys of life, falls into the snare
of spiritual pride, the brave and healthy
lover, in the person of Farina, escapes and
succeeds. As the second last paragraph of
the conclusion hints, the final victory over
conceit is gained by true love. Meredith here
draws a burlesque vignette of what reappears
in tragic and comic shapes on almost every
one of his later and larger canvases.

THE ORDEAL
OF RICHARD FEVEREL

The Ordeal of Richard Feverel

THE sub-title of this novel, which was published in 1859, is "A History of Father and Son." It is a study of the Egoist as father, and of a son who has the misfortune to be the victim of a paternal system. When Meredith wrote this novel, the romantic movement was beginning to give way before the scientific; fresh ideas about evolution, heredity, and environment were in the air; and Herbert Spencer had just published in the "British Quarterly Review" (April, 1858) his famous essay upon the place of natural reactions in education, contending that parents ought to let their children feel the true consequences of their conduct, and pleading among other things that "in its injurious effects on both parent and child a bad system is twice cursed." Like Austin Caxton and Mr. Shandy, Sir Austin Feverel has a system of

his own, but it is the system of a benevolent
despot who exaggerates his parental re-
sponsibilities.* His aim is to shut out the
world from the tender plant, to repress some
of the more natural instincts, and to bend the
twig into the shape of his own personality.
The consequences of this system form the
contents of the story.

Like George Eliot, Meredith had tried his
'prentice hand in short stories before he
published his first masterpiece. The "Scenes
of Clerical Life," written contemporaneously
with "Shagpat" and "Farina," gave far
more promise of "Adam Bede," however,
than Meredith's first stories did of "The
Ordeal of Richard Feverel." When Lewes
read "Amos Barton," he told George Eliot,
"I think your pathos is better than your
fun." "Shagpat" and "Farina" are full of
fun. Pathos is not in them. No reader of
these *jeux d'esprit* could expect anything like
the imaginative power, the penetration into
human nature, the combination of sombre

* There is an excellent statement of this error, in the sphere of
political despotism, by Mr. Chesterton in his sentences on Strafford
("Browning," p. 31).

pathos and brilliant comedy, which "The
Ordeal of Richard Feverel" presented.

There should be a Society for the Protection of Books against their Authors. This
novel is one of those which have suffered
from revision ; it has been repeatedly pruned
by Meredith, and not always with discretion.
If he had applied his knife to a book like
"One of Our Conquerors," it would have
been more to the point. As it is, a reader of
the earlier editions may congratulate himself
upon the fact that their defects in *format* are
more than counterbalanced by their un-
thinned chapters. The alterations, however,
have not affected the essentials of the plot,
which works out as follows.

Sir Austin Feverel, of Raynham Abbey,
had been deserted by his wife, who eloped
five years after their marriage with his
friend Denzil Somers. Somers, a minor
poet whose pseudonym was Diaper Sandoe,
"being inclined to vice, and occasionally, and
in a quiet way, practising it, was of course a
sentimentalist and a satirist, entitled to lash
the Age and complain of human nature."
The moral tone of his poems was unex-

ceptional. But he deceived his friend and patron, and, after playing Rizzio to Lady Feverel's Mary, carried off the pretty, inexperienced woman to a life of disenchantment and privation. The two hardly appear upon the stage of the story. Lady Feverel steals in once or twice to get a glimpse of her boy, and Somers stoops to ask an annuity from Sir Austin. But the latter despised his former friend too much to seek any revenge, though he was incapable of forgiving the wound dealt his pride by his wife.* To their only child Sir Austen devotes himself with a fussy, fingering attention. He has a cherished system of education for the boy, based half on pride and half on sentimentalism. Convinced that schools and colleges were corrupt, he aims at playing Providence himself. He wishes to direct every move in the lad's moral and mental development. "If immeasurable love were perfect wisdom, one human being might almost impersonate Providence to another." But the very ordeal

* Sir Austin, however, is not vindictive. The twist given to his bruised heart produces simply a suspicion of women—one of the sources to which Meredith is fond of tracing the aberrations of men.

of Richard arises from his father's well-meant, unwise endeavour to confine natural tendencies within the artificial restraints of a preconceived theory. This in ordinary circumstances would turn out a prig or a rake. Which will Richard be? Or, is he to be either?

The novel opens on the boy's fourteenth birthday, when he and his companion, Ripton Thompson, the son of Sir Austin's solicitor, are horsewhipped by a certain Farmer Blaize for poaching and trespassing. In order to revenge themselves, the boys persuade a country lad, Tom Bakewell, to set fire that evening to the farmer's ricks. Tom is arrested and imprisoned, to the consternation of the lads, whose plot is found out by the baronet and his circle. Finally, after considerable manœuvring on the part of various members of the family, the yokel is acquitted, but not until Richard has had to apologise humbly to the farmer.* His conquest of pride appears to his father a fresh

---

* Austin Wentworth, whose influence helps Richard here as in the end of the tale, partly belongs to the class of Vernon Whitford, partly to that of Dartrey Fenellan. Adrian Harley ranks with Colney Durance, no higher.

George Meredith

proof of the correctness of the system. The small dose of the world, for which poor Ripton is blamed, has turned out well, the baronet reflects, owing to the excellent way in which Richard has been trained.

The second stage of the ordeal, however, is more serious and less satisfactory. During the next four years, the baronet's main anxiety is to keep all ideas of love away from the lad's mind. The preliminary blossoming season, as he terms it, when conscience and mind have to be awakened, passes safely, though Richard is on the fair way to become a little prig.* The only bad omen is an attack of scribbling. Sir Austin, however, gets the boy to burn his verses. "He drew out bundle after bundle: each neatly tied, named, and numbered ; and pitched them into flames. And so farewell my young Ambition ! and with it farewell all true confidence between Father and Son." Sir Austin is blissfully unconscious of this error. He congratulates himself on having

* His intercourse with Ralph Morton knocks manliness into him: but, if it hits a wholesome stroke at his vanity, it also fosters the disposition to love. For Ralph is in the first stages of a boyish passion for Clare Doria Forey.

The Ordeal of Richard Feverel

a pure and obedient boy, and now proceeds to safeguard his treasure against the temptations of the Magnetic age. His precautions border on the ludicrous. All servants at the Abbey who show any visible symptoms of the tender passion are at once dismissed, thanks mainly to the efforts of heavy Benson, the butler; Clare Doria Forey, Richard's little cousin, has to leave the Abbey with her mother; and Sir Austin proceeds to London in order to look out a suitable wife for his young hopeful. Richard is eighteen; he is to marry, acccording to the system, at the age of twenty-five.

But the schemes of baronets as well as of mice "gang aft a-gley." Like Pisistratus Caxton, Richard is already at school with the two great teachers, Nature and Love. He has chosen his mate, by falling in love with Lucy Desborough, the seventeen-year old niece of Farmer Blaize. Adrian Feverel, his uncle and tutor, finds out the secret; Benson, the butler, writes to Sir Austin; and Richard is inveigled up to town by a false report of his father's illness. He soon discovers that Sir Austin is not only perfectly well but quite aware of the engagement. His father's thinly-veiled advice and sarcasms destroy any chance of confidences being exchanged between the two, but Richard is kept dangling for three weeks beside him, until Adrian and Lady Blandish (a sentimental widow, who is in Sir Austin's confidence) get the farmer to pack off Lucy back to her French school. Richard returns to the Abbey and falls ill, only to recover from his physical and apparently from his amorous malady.* The following March, as he accompanies one of his uncles to London, he happens to hear that Lucy is coming home to be married to young Tom Blaize, the farmer's son—an arrangement which had been carefully concealed from him. The love-passion revives at once. He meets her, places her, with the aid of Ripton, under the care of a Mrs. Berry in lodgings, and then marries her secretly. Miranda is rescued from the Caliban who threatened to be her fate, and Ferdinand is the rescuer.

---

* Meredith here and elsewhere is careful to note the effects produced by physical illness upon the spirit of his men and women.

The Ordeal of Richard Feverel

Sir Austin blames neither himself[*] nor the system, but his son, whom he moodily reproaches for treachery and deception. The baronet nurses the devil of his wounded pride. His conceit is unbroken; he will not admit the possibility of any error in the experiment which he has been practising on his boy. Beyond making him an allowance, he declines to take any notice of the marriage, shutting his heart against his only son. This bitter attitude leaves Richard sad and angry, and Lucy rather depressed. What Richard wants is not money, but a kind word from his father, which the latter, in his cold superiority and unnatural reserve, will not stoop to bestow.

Meantime the young couple at the Isle of Wight are in dangerous company. Richard, for the first time, is meeting men and women in free intercourse, including a Lord Mountfalcon and a dark, tall, attractive Lady

---

[*] The irony of the business is that Richard's instinct of love is vaguely stirred first of all by witnessing his father's lordly philandering with Lady Blandish. Benson, who spies another instance of this, is finally dismissed for his inquisitiveness, but not before he has been flogged by Richard for intruding upon the privacy of the younger lovers. The amorous Curate, who has strayed in from the pages of "Pendennis" is an even milder figure than his fellow in "The Adventures of Harry Richmond."

Judith Felle. The former is a villain, the latter a sentimental married woman. By the diplomacy of Adrian and Lady Blandish, Richard is persuaded to come alone to London, in the hope that Sir Austin may consent at least to see him, if not to take him back. Adrian persuades Lucy to agree to this sacrifice, and even to urge it, arguing that this is in Richard's interest ; the young husband, though accusing her of cowardice and unable to understand her real motive, falls in with his uncle's plan. Mrs. Doria Forey further persuades him, after Clare's marriage, to wait for his father in London, unless he wishes to make Sir Austin marry Lady Blandish. Sir Austin's real aim, however, is to separate husband and wife. His angry temper has devised this punishment for Richard ; the latter, wishing to humour and manage his father, and ignorant of the dastardly plot, remains in the metropolis, where another plot is laid against him and Lucy. He is inveigled by a Mrs. Mountstuart, acting under the instructions of Lord Mountfalcon, who has designs upon poor Lucy at the Isle of Wight.

The Ordeal of Richard Feverel

Richard's impulse of chivalry* leads him to champion the reputation of this woman, and also to rescue his mother from the life she was living. He summons Lucy, but she—misled by Adrian—thinks she will make the family feel her worth more by patiently waiting where she is, in case the baronet should feel aggrieved by any sudden move upon his privacy. The result is that Richard, in a moment of disappointment with her, flings himself recklessly into Mrs. Mountstuart's company, and is carried further than he meant.

Meantime, Sir Austin's pride has begun to relent towards his son and daughter-in-law. He had gone off with a note-book to write aphorisms in Wales, but has now returned. Only, his amendment is too late. † Richard receives his father's tentative

---

* The first ebullition of this quixotic instinct broke out in his attempt to hinder the loveless marriage which was being forced on his cousin Clare. This was one of the reasons which hurried him up to London. The second course of folly was due to his ignorance of the world (one result of the system) and his vanity. Sir Austin has told Adrian to let Richard see the world, this being partly designed as an education, partly in order to keep him away from Lucy.

† Meredith here touches the string which we shall find sounding loudly in " Rhoda Fleming," " Lord Ormont and his Aminta," and " The Amazing Marriage."

George Meredith

advances coldly ; black shame keeps him from joining Lucy, whom he has wronged ; and, as Sir Austin refuses to receive her at the Abbey without him, matters are at a stand-still. Richard, cursing himself for his folly, goes off to the Continent, where he joins the sentimental Lady Felle, while Lucy, whom Mrs. Berry has rescued from her aristocratic admirer, gives birth to a child in London. At this point, Austin Wentworth, one of Richard's uncles, a quiet, strong, chivalrous gentleman, returns from abroad, and intervenes. He takes Lucy and her baby to Raynham Abbey, where the baronet capitulates at sight to the girl-wife's charm. Then he fetches Richard home from Nassau in the Rhine-land, after hard persuasion, by telling him the amazing news of his father-hood. "He felt in his heart the cry of his child, his darling's touch. With shut eyes he saw them both. They drew him from the depths ; they led him a blind and tottering man. And as they led him he had a sense of purification so sweet he shuddered again and again."

All is now going well, and Richard is

The Ordeal of Richard Feverel

hurrying home, when in passing through London he happens to hear of Lord Mountfalcon's infamous and unsuccessful plot against his wife, which had been the cause of his degradation. The lad's hot blood is up. He challenges the aristocrat to a duel, feeling that he must take vengeance on the villain and clear his personal honour * before he can settle down with Lucy. A hurried visit to Raynham Abbey follows ; he tears himself from his wife and child, after a heartrending scene, and is severely wounded in France by his opponent. He recovers, only to be told that Lucy, who had crossed to nurse him, had died of brain fever.

When the novel had been published, James Thomson told his friend frankly that no woman, and scarcely any man, would ever forgive him for "the cruel, cruel ending." Lucy's death is one of the few blots in the book, and the objections to it are not to be

---

* Thus it is false or wounded pride which wrecks the son, as, in a different form, it was a mixture of pride and vanity which had warped the father. "A mad pleasure in the prospect of wreaking vengeance on the villain who had laid the trap for him, once more blackened his brain." In the instant when he confesses to Lucy that he had been a vain fool, he is still yielding, as Meredith observes, to "the powers of hell."

bundled aside as so many weak cravings for the sugar-plum ending. It is not required by the system, and it is even more inartistic* than the drowning of Beauchamp. The girl's character is described, otherwise, with singular precision, from the day when, as a pretty little child of thirteen, she sees the handsome, sulky boy coming to apologize to her uncle, down to the ripening of her nature through marriage and motherhood. She is young, even when she dies, but never insipid for an instant. Her sweet womanliness, even more than her beauty, is the clue to the charm which she exercises on the Feverels. She is the sort of girl Meredith paints in "Marian," except that she never dealt "a wound that lingers." There is just a suspicion of unreality in Meredith's account of her relations with Lord Mountfalcon; her innocence and simplicity are too credulous. Even her subservience to Adrian's influence is left half-explained. But whenever she is

---

* The shadow of the cypress (in chapter xxi) may be intended as a preliminary hint, but Lucy's pretty fear of it only came after Richard has scattered her anxieties about his father. The tree is too subtle to bear the weight of a premonition.

106

The Ordeal of Richard Feverel

with Richard the sheer loveliness of her nature breaks through.*

Mrs. Berry takes us to her capacious heart from the moment when we go with Richard to her lodgings at West Kensington. She proves a shrewd and kind and homely nurse to Lucy. But she also reads Sir Austin's character and speaks to him bravely when she gets the chance. Her talk† has the plain sense and wit of Mrs. Poyser's, and she richly deserves the return of her erring Berry towards the novel's close. She had been a cook at Raynham, from which she had been exiled on a small pension for having assisted once to carry Adrian drunk to bed; the baronet's pride could not endure the presence of this witness to his relative's offence. Her revenge came to her unsought in the services she chanced to render to Richard and Lucy against Sir Austin's will. She thereby became an unconscious agent in upsetting the baronet's system.

* She has French blood in her veins, though her father was an English naval officer.

† "Don't neglect your cookery. Kissing don't last: cookery do." "One gets so addle-pated thinkin' many things. That's why we see wonder clever people al'ays goin' wrong—to my mind. I think it's al'ays the plan in a dielemmer to pray God and walk forward."

107

George Meredith

The baronet, like Sir Willoughby Patterne, is further punished by the fact that the woman, on whose admiration he counted, comes to see through him. Lady Blandish ceases to be a worshipper and is forced to become a critic. The book ends with a letter to Austin Wentworth, which voices her vehement contempt for Sir Austin and his mad self-deceit.* Meredith characteristically traces this infatuation in large measure to his lack of humour. "The faculty of laughter was denied him. A good wind of laughter had relieved him of much of the blight of self-deception, and oddness, and extravagance ; had given a healthier view of our atmosphere of life ; but he had it not." This was the philosophy† which afterwards appeared in the ode "To the Comic Spirit." As Meredith notes, even Richard and Lucy could laugh, in the dawn of their love-passion ; which proves that their feelings were not

* Adrian Feverel, the wise youth, whose satirical wisdom proves so ineffective, is guilty of the same error. "The wise youth's two ears were stuffed with his own wisdom."

† Fielding has a touch of it in the fourth paragraph of his invocation in "Tom Jones" (book xiii, ch. i).

The Ordeal of Richard Feverel

sentimental rouge. "Better than sentiment, laughter opens the breast to love."

Ripton, for all his peccadilloes,* shows that the normal training of youth is healthier than the system of Sir Austin. For one thing, Ripton, like Shibli and Pisistratus Caxton, has known what it is to be thwacked. Richard had missed the wholesome birchings of school, but his friend was familiar with the rod. "He was seasoned wood, and took the world pretty wisely; not reckless of castigation, as some boys become, nor over-sensitive to dishonour, as his friend and comrade beside him was." His humble, adoring devotion for Lucy, which is one with his loyalty to Richard, shows the good heart in him. "He had the Old Dog's eyes in his head. They watched the door she had passed through; they listened for her, as dogs' eyes do. When she hung on her lover timidly, and went forth, he followed without an idea of envy, or anything save the secret raptures the sight of her

* The law of gavelkind which he uses as a feint (in ch. xiv), was a Saxon custom, surviving in Wales and Kent, by which primogeniture was set aside in favour of an equal distribution of property, at a man's death, among his sons and daughters.

George Meredith

gave him, which are the Old Dog's own. His sensations cannot be heroic, but they have a fulness, and a wagging delight, as good in their way."*

The variety of power in the novel is illustrated by the typical chapters, "Ferdinand and Miranda"† and "A Diversion played on a Penny-Whistle," which breathe the spirit of "Love in a Valley"; the successive episodes of the marriage, including the rather broad farce of Ripton's hilarious conduct, which is on much the same level as the chapters entitled "A Dinner Party at Richmond" and "An Enchantress"; the account of Clare's diary (which verges on the sentimental); and the agonizing interview of the penultimate chapter. Twice, when Richard finds Lucy beside the river, and when he hears that he is a father (in the chapter, "Nature Speaks"), Meredith reproduces the wonderful rhythm

* Carinthia, at the end of "The Amazing Marriage," accepted Wythan because he wooed her "with dog's eyes instead of words."

† The paragraph which closes the chapter immediately before, and which describes Richard coming upon Lucy by the river's edge, is full of the colour and fragrance which had already been felt in some of the early poems. In his next novel, Meredith almost repeated this success in the description of Rose and Evan beside the stream, but the lovers there do not flash on one another with the thrill of their predecessors.

The Ordeal of Richard Feverel

of nature with the moods and passions of the soul which was always a characteristic feature alike of his prose and of his verse.

Meredith's device for floating his epigrams in this novel is "The Pilgrim's Scrip," which is supposed to be a volume of aphorisms published by the baronet. These are couched sometimes in a deliberately commonplace shape, but now and then the author stamps himself upon a phrase, as in the following instances: "The compensation for injustice is, that in that dark ordeal we gather the worthiest around us." "Who rises from prayer a better man, his prayer *is* answered." "Who can say when he is not walking a puppet to some woman?"* "Sentimentalists are they who seek to enjoy without incurring the Immense Debtorship for a thing done." "Give me purity to be worthy the good in her, and grant her patience to reach the good in me" (the lover's petition). The baronet, however, did not like his aphorisms to be criticised or questioned; they were to be taken as oracles; even "the direct application of

* This is expounded in "Evan Harrington" (see the close of chapter xviii).

111

George Meredith

an aphorism was unpopular at Raynham."
"The Pilgrim's Scrip" and several episodes
show that the author is a trifle conscious of
his powers, but the scheme and style of the
novel prove that the powers are there, even
though sometimes they are devoted to the
splitting of psychological seeds. One outstanding feature is the maturity of conception
which is displayed in the treatment of the
leading characters. The motive-grinding,
which is audible in several of the later novels,
has already begun, but this is a defect of the
writer's strength as a watcher of the deep
moods of the human soul.

Note, by the way, (*a*) the satirical allusion
to Richardson's hero at the opening of the
nineteenth chapter, where the author also
describes Mrs. Caroline Grandison who bore
eight daughters in succession, and then,
despairing of a son, "relapsed upon religion
and little dogs." She was "a colourless lady
of an unequivocal character, living upon
drugs, and governing her husband and the
world from her sofa. Woolly negroes blest
her name, and whiskered John-Thomases de-
plored her weight." A sister of Mrs. Jellyby!

The Ordeal of Richard Feverel

(*b*) The paragraph on snobbery in chapter xxxv ("The Conquest of an Epicure"), with its thesis that "the national love of a lord is less subservience than a form of self-love," was echoed, years later, by Ruskin in his "Fors Clavigera" (letter lxiii) criticism of Thackeray, whom he accused of being blind to the fact that "it is *himself* the snob truly worships, all the time, and not the Lord he looks at." (*c*) Sir F. C. Burnand, in his "Records and Reminiscences," recalled the figure of Maurice Fitzgerald, an eccentric epicure and scholar, whom Meredith used to call "the wise youth." The novelist, however, repudiated the inference that Fitzgerald was the prototype of Adrian Harley. Fitzgerald was neither selfish nor unprincipled. It is needless to do more than mention, as a curiosity of error, the idea that Adrian is meant to represent the author's characteristic attitude towards life. (*d*) Boiardo and Berni, whom Lady Blandish included in her studies of literature, were two Italian poets. The former a distinguished scholar of the fifteenth century, wrote an "Orlando Innamorato," which formed the basis of Ariosto's more famous

H 113

poem. Berni, who was a comic poet of the next century, edited and recast Boiardo's romantic epic. Meredith more than once alludes to them, as Peacock had already done.

Finally the novel is remarkable as containing a defence, by way of anticipation, of the psychological, introspective method upon which the author proposed to write. "At present, I am aware, an audience impatient for blood and glory scorns the stress I am putting on incidents so minute, a picture so little imposing. An audience will come"—it has come, but not nearly so soon as the writer perhaps expected or certainly deserved—"to whom it will be given to see the elementary machinery at work: who, as it were, from some slight hint of the straws, will feel the winds of March when they do not blow . . . And they will perceive, moreover, that in real life all hangs together: the train is laid in the lifting of an eyebrow, that bursts upon the field of thousands." Nineteen years passed before a second edition of the novel was required. But Meredith persisted in his chosen course, though, five years later, he recognised in "Sandra Belloni" with a wry, impenitent air that the philosophic digressions were resented in fiction : " and away flies my book back at the heads of the librarians, hitting me behind them a far more grievous blow." He answers his critics not only, like Terence and Fielding, in prologues but in unexpected places, and the answer usually heralds a fresh offence. Still Meredith, even in his irrelevance, might have safely pled with Montaigne : " 'Tis the indifferent reader that loses my subject, not I ; there will always be found some words or other in a corner that are to the purpose."

The minor characters include specimens of the modern equivalents of the parasite and the *demi-monde* which social comedy had retained since the days of Menander. Mrs. Mount's type re-appears in Mrs. Marsett in " One of our Conquerors," though the setting is different, and the parasite of Lord Mount-falcon ranks with Captain Cumnock in "Lord Ormont and his Aminta" and with the toadies of Lord Fleetwood in " The Amazing Marriage." The book further gives proof of Meredith's ability to describe the life of the English upper classes, especially in country houses—a department in which both Dickens and Richardson before him had rarely shown themselves at home. The later novels, particularly "The Egoist" and "Beauchamp's Career," exhibit still happier results in this line. Fielding once attributed to ignorance the failure of many English novelists to describe the manners of good society. Oddly enough, he confided to his readers (in "Tom Jones," book xiv, ch. i) that such a knowledge of upper life "is no very great resource to a writer whose province is comedy or that kind of novel which is of the comic class." Meredith's conception of the Comic Spirit led him to a very different opinion, as his next novel was to show.

EVAN HARRINGTON

Evan Harrington

THE sub-title of this novel, as it appeared serially in "Once a Week," during 1860, was : "He would be a Gentleman." It really puts, in the form of a social comedy, some aspects of the question which Ruskin raised simultaneously in the fifth volume of his "Modern Painters"—the question, what constitutes a gentleman on the one hand and vulgarity on the other ? Both Ruskin and Meredith attacked the conventional English idea that a gentleman is one who lives in idleness, upon the fruits of other people's labour, and the equally absurd notion that birth and blood are of no account. Ruskin analysed vulgarity into callousness, suspiciousness, cruelty, and meanness, as the expression of indifference to the interests of other people ; its reverse side was an undue regard to appearances and manners, and "the assumption of behaviour, language, or dress

George Meredith

unsuited to them, by persons in inferior stations of life." Sensitiveness of feeling, sympathy, and self-command, he noted among the traits of the essential gentleman. Newman, eight years before,[*] had essayed to define a gentleman in " The Idea of a University "—the most versatile and permanent of all his works. His definition of good breeding suffers from undue restriction. Its main element is the refusal to inflict pain. But consideration for the feelings of others at all costs would rule out gentlemen from a number of useful professions ; besides, the essence of a gentleman is to remember not only what is due to others but to himself. Meredith's analysis, as given in this novel of manners, is that to be a gentleman is inconsistent, not with trade but with pretence of any kind, and that the primary requisites are sincerity and courage. When T. H. Green opened the Oxford High School, he closed his address with these words : " As it was the aspiration of Moses that all the Lord's people should be prophets, so with all serious-

* " John Halifax, Gentleman," Miss Mulock's masterpiece, had appeared in 1856.

ness and reverence we may hope and pray for a condition of English Society in which all honest citizens will recognise themselves and be recognised by others as gentlemen." Meredith's contribution to this end, in "Evan Harrington," was to hold up to ridicule false gentility and sham social pretensions; he took a tailor as his hero, and used the Comic Spirit to illustrate his philosophy of society. In "Sandra Belloni," three years later, he touched on the same problem incidentally. But "Evan Harrington" was his full-dress exposition of the theme, in semi-comic guise.

If it is true that Meredith's father [*] was a naval outfitter at Portsmouth and that Melchisedec was the name of the author's grandfather, we might be justified in spying behind this story as we do behind "David Copperfield." But its intrinsic merits are independent of this attraction. The outline of the tale, as told by Meredith, is this:—

Melchisedec Harrington, a tailor, at Lym-

[*] The story goes that once, on a visit to Bath, he was taken for a foreign Count in disguise (see ch. i). When the story appeared, he was a tailor in Capetown, and resented his son's use of the paternal exploits.

port-on-the-Sea, "whom people in private called the great Mel, had been at once the sad dog of Lymport, and the pride of the town. He was a tailor, and he kept horses ; he was a tailor, and he had gallant adventures ; he was a tailor, and he shook hands with his customers." He had married a strong, sensible woman, Henrietta Maria Dawley, by whom he had four children, three daughters and one son. Mel's great aim and pleasure was to move in county society, where he was welcomed for his gay wit and manners, particularly as these were coupled with a strong sense of personal honour. Mel never cringed or sailed under false colours. "He was a robust Brummel, and the Regent of low life," who was respected by his betters, in spite of his snobbish tastes. "Combine—say Mirabeau and Alcibiades, and the result is the Lymport tailor :—he measures your husband in the morning : in the evening he makes love to you, through a series of pantomimic transformations. He was a colossal Adonis." Mel fostered the same tastes in his family. He read heraldry with his daughters, and saw them all make good matches. The

eldest of them, Caroline, married Major
Strike ; the second, Harriet, was won by a
wealthy London brewer, Mr. Andrew
Cogglesby ; while the third, Louisa, became
the wife of a Portuguese diplomatist, Señor
Silva Diaz, Conde de Saldar. The husband
of the eldest daughter knew the trade of his
father-in-law ; Mr. Cogglesby came to suspect
it in due time ; but the Count was kept in ignorance. All three wives agreed, however, to
avoid the neighbourhood of Lymport. Caroline, a weak and pretty woman, had the
hardest lot. She had married a military
edition of Quilp. "If we may be permitted
to suppose the colonel of a regiment on
friendly terms with one of his corporals, we
have an estimate of the domestic life of Major
and Mrs. Strike." Harriet had a good
husband, a large family, and plenty of money.
Louisa had no money, but then she had no
children and her husband was a puppet whom
she had met under Harriet's auspices. She
was the pushful, independent genius of the
family, and it was she who headed the
enterprise of rescuing Evan, their brother,
from the bondage of tailordom. He was to

be a soldier, and meantime he "spent the hours not devoted to his positive profession — that of gentleman — in the offices of the brewery, toying with big books and balances which he despised with the combined zeal of the sucking soldier and emancipated tailor." The Countess determined to furnish him with money, if not with a title ; she took him to Portugal to meet Rose Jocelyn, the niece of the British representative there. Rose had the prospects of an heiress, and Evan was to marry money in her person.

The story opens with the return of the Countess, her husband and brother, and Miss Jocelyn, in the company of the Hon. Melville Jocelyn, the diplomatist. Rose and Evan are already close friends, and the aim of the Countess is to secure an invitation for all her party to Beckley Court, in Hampshire, the seat of the Jocelyns, where she hopes to bring off the engagement ; Beckley Court is not far from Lymport, but she is resolved to take the risks of its proximity to tailordom. They are met at London by the news of the great Mel's death. Evan alone goes down to the

Evan Harrington

funeral.* He finds that the evil that men do
lives after them. The great Mel has left a
mass of debts, which Mrs. Harrington determines her son is to clear off. He shares this
honourable impulse. He is willing enough to
enter the business and devote himself to this
enterprise. But his father has left another
legacy, in the shape of the false ambitions and
ideals which he had instilled into his children.
Evan is still susceptible to these, and the
interest of his career now centres upon the
uncertainty as to which course he is strong
enough to choose and to keep. Under the
influence of his mother's determination, he
decides manfully to clear his father's name,
and, with a view to this, to serve in the London
shop. But his sisters have other views. The
Countess descends upon Lymport, and,
although unable to intercept Evan's flight,
manages to catch him at a cricket-match and
draw him in her train to Beckley Court, where
Sir Frank and Lady Jocelyn welcome them as
friends of their daughter Rose. Meantime,

* The description of his journey and his postillion, in ch. iv, is
Meredith's first essay in the "open-road adventures" which he afterwards
reproduced in "Diana of the Crossways,";"Lord Ormont and his
Aminta," and "The Amazing Marriage."

George Meredith

however, Evan has publicly called himself a tailor * in the hearing of some young men at an inn who chanced to quarrel with him and an eccentric friend, John Raikes. These youths include Harry, a brother of Rose, and Ferdinand Laxley, an aristocratic suitor for her hand. They are naturally amazed to find the "tailor" a fellow-guest at Beckley Court, but the Countess, by consummate intriguing, manages to allay their suspicions for a time. She enjoys the sense of rank at Beckley ; a visit there gratifies what had been one of her girlish dreams. But the main object of her generalship is to bring Rose and Evan together, and Beckley is the vantage-ground for the engagement. Rose, who loves Evan, has begun already to suspect he is a tradesman, and the persistent hints dropped by Laxley and the rest confirm her idea. Evan, under the delightful influence of her charm, is beginning to forget his vows to tailordom ; his surroundings threaten to soften the fibre of his resolve. But meantime Mr. Tom Cogglesby, the eccen-

* " He gathered his pride as a cloak, and defied the world, and gloried in the sacrifice that degraded him." Later on, a similar infusion of false pride spoils his honourable conduct in assuming responsibility for the forged letter.

Evan Harrington

tric brother of Andrew, proposes anonymously
to pay him £360 a year, as soon as he puts his
name over the shop in Lymport. This offer
recalls Evan to his senses, and, by the medium
of Mr. John Raikes,* he accepts it. The die
now seems cast. But the spell of Rose is not
so easily broken ; he learns from her maid
that she suspects his trade, and, letting his
anger at Laxley get the better of his prudence,
he calls himself a "gentleman," intending, in
all sincerity, to leave Beckley for London the
next day. The wily Countess proves too
many for him, however. She works on his
love for Mrs. Strike, who has come to Beckley
to escape further ill-treatment at the Major's
hands. He must not leave her unprotected !
Both sisters have to suffer torture in listening
to tales of the great Mel told by unconscious
guests in the house, but Evan is made
happy by confessing his love to Rose and
winning hers in return. He then summons
up courage to write a letter to her, telling her

---

* Raikes has been heavily criticised. Henley asserted that he and
Dr. Shrapnel were "two of the most flagrant unrealities ever perpetrated
in the name of fiction by an artist of genius." Shrapnel may be left behind.
He is little more than a seven-foot funnel for Meredith's social philosophy.
But Raikes has blood in him—the blood of Dickens.

frankly the whole truth about his birth and position. The Countess steals the letter, and Evan, supposing that Rose has received it, is relieved to find she makes no change in her bearing to him. Rose then tells her mother about her engagement, but is staggered, a moment afterwards, to learn from some of the guests that her lover is a tailor, with his name over a shop in Lymport. Rose now has to face her ordeal. Evan's insinuations had wakened her suspicions even in Portugal, and the scene on board the ship—when the great Mel's foreman, in announcing his death, had mentioned the fatal word "shop"—had half confirmed her suspicions. But her love had hitherto felt itself strong enough to conquer such prejudices. The actual news, however, fills her with a sick despair ; it looks as if Evan had wooed her under false pretences. Evan at once clears himself of duplicity * by telling her orally what he had written to her in the purloined letter, and

* Rose, like Princess Ottilia in "The Adventures of Harry Richmond," can bear anything except concealment or dishonesty (ch. xxvii). Evan's frankness "hurried her spirit out of all shows and forms, and habits of thought, up to the gates of existence, as it were, where she took him simply as God had created him and her, and clave to him" (ch. xxviii).

Evan Harrington

Rose, sure of his candour, has now to struggle against the class-prejudices of a girl who finds herself engaged to one who is socially her inferior. "It was some time before she was was able to get free from the trammels of prejudice, but when she did, she did without reserve, saying : 'Evan, there is no man who would have done so much,' and he was told that he was better loved than ever."

The troubles of the lovers are not yet over, however. Mrs. Harrington, on hearing that Evan was idling at a country-house instead of attending to his business in London, starts for Beckley to bring her son to his senses. *En route* she falls in with the eccentric Tom Cogglesby, who also is on his way to visit Lady Jocelyn* and to ascertain the conduct of the youth who had bound himself to tailordom. Old Tom promises her ladyship to endow Evan with a thousand a year at least, if Rose is allowed to marry him, but the

---

* "Was it true that her ladyship had behaved rather ill to old Tom in her youth? Excellent women have been naughty girls, and young beauties will have their train. It is also very possible that old Tom had presumed upon trifles and found it difficult to forgive her his own folly" (ch. xxviii). He had attributed her rejection of him to the fact that he was a cobbler's son ; hence he takes a revenge in furthering Rose's marriage to a tailor !

George Meredith

Jocelyns disapprove of the match, and Mrs.
Mel appears at a picnic to claim her tailor-son
for the career to which he had pledged his
honour. The Countess, exasperated at her
brother and her mother, has meantime taken
her revenge on Laxley by forging a letter in his
name. (She had found, on looking at Rose's
album, that Laxley's writing resembled her
own.) Evan, on discovering this trick,
quixotically assumes responsibility for the
letter, in order to shield his sister's name.
His engagement is at once broken off, and the
three Harringtons leave Beckley Court.
Rose is stunned by the revelation of what
appears to be Evan's low-bred deceit, and the
only person who disbelieves in his confession
is Juliana Bonner, the sickly little heiress of
the Court, who has a morbid, romantic, and
unrequited passion for him.

Thus ends the fourth act of the comedy.
Evan now becomes a tailor in London ; he
is done with Beckley and its inmates. But
the Countess, with the aid of her sisters,
continues to keep up a correspondence with
Juliana, in order to bring the latter and Evan
together and so win Beckley Court in the

end. Rose is out of the question; she has practically pledged herself to Laxley, and besides she is no longer the heiress. Juliana dies, however, and to the consternation of the Jocelyns, she is found to have bequeathed Beckley Court and all her property "to Mr. Evan Harrington, of Lymport, tailor." The Countess is overjoyed, but her triumph is short-lived. Evan rises to the occasion. He chivalrously renounces the estate. "Upon my honour," says Sir Franks, " he must have the soul of a gentleman ! There's nothing he can expect in return, you know !" Whatever Evan may have expected, he at any rate wins Rose ; for, when the Jocelyns go to Lymport, to thank him for his generosity, she hears from his own lips * the true tale of the Laxley-letter, and the lovers come together. The curtain falls on the hero as attaché to the Naples embassy.

"Most youths are like Pope's women ; they have no character at all." This verdict of Meredith is truer of Wilfrid Pole and Harry Richmond than of Evan. Like the latter he is managed by stronger influences ; indeed

* Juliana had left her the news as a bitter legacy.

George Meredith

Roy Richmond's intriguing filled Ottilia with much the same disgust as the Countess de Saldar's vulgar scheming threatened to stir in the honest Rose, who was tempted to think hardly of a brother who had such a sister for his ally. But Evan has fibre and grit in him. Besides, he is steadied by his true love for Rose as well as by the determined honesty of his mother, which saves him at the expense of his dignity. Love furnishes the real ordeal, however, and it brings out the best as well as the worst in him, purifying the latter. The hinge of the plot is, will Evan be a man, as well as a gentleman? He has the makings of the latter, and, once his early weakness and false pride * are overcome, he regains his self-respect and, with it, his moral force of character.

Rose's conduct from the moment of Evan's confession becomes rather unconvincing, and the end of the story is huddled up, as too often happens in Meredith; the lovers are flung together by a sort of accident. But the courage of her love entitles her to happiness. She

* "Pride was the one developed faculty of Evan's nature. The Fates who mould us, always work from the mainspring" (ch. vi).

132

masters the fear of ridicule as Evan does in
his own way. Love had set for her as for
him a moral test, even though the details of
the test seem paltry enough. She had to decide "whether it was really in Nature's power,
unaided by family-portraits, coats-of-arms,
ball-room practice, and at least one small
phial of essence of society, to make a gentleman." By her truthfulness to the facts of
life, she wins clear of the unrealities and conventions which beset her position, and thus,
unlike Ottilia, retains her lover. At the same
time her task must be admitted to have been
easier in some respects than that of the German
princess; Evan could play the second fiddle
better than Harry Richmond ever learnt to
do, and besides the social gulf between Rose
and Evan was more easily bridged than in
the case of the other pair.

But the glory—though it is a spotted glory—
of the novel is the character of the Countess,
a superb adventuress, with her sentimental
aspirations for society, her vulgarity, and her
unscrupulous scheming. *Tous les comédiens
ne sont pas au théâtre.* The Countess is an
actress of high rank in the social comedy.

George Meredith

She might have stepped out of Thackeray's pages, but, while Becky Sharp fights for her own hand, the Countess has a larger scheme in view ; she is bent on carrying her family, especially her brother, out of the cold shades of Tailordom into the warm paradise of Society. The Comic Spirit revels in her, and Meredith lets her reveal herself in letters as well as in conversation. "I hope I shall be pardoned," she writes, "but it *always* seems to me that what *we* have to endure is infinitely worse than any other suffering, for you find no comfort for the children of T—s in Scripture, nor any defence of their dreadful position. Robbers, thieves, Magdalens ! but, no ! the unfortunate offspring of that class are not even mentioned ; at least, in my most diligent perusal of the Scriptures, I never lighted upon any remote allusion, and we know the Jews did wear clothing." Her nauseous affectation of religion prepares us for her final move into the Roman Church where she finds gentility *

* The sentimental Cornelia Pole, in "Sandra Belloni" (ch. xvii), sighs over Mrs. Chump : "Do you know, my feeling is, and I cannot at all account for it, that if she were a Catholic, she would not seem so gross." Constance Asper thought of becoming a nun when Percy seemed to jilt her for Diana Warwick.

and peace of mind—a proceeding which here, as in "The Amazing Marriage," Meredith traces to rank sentimentalism. "It is the sweet sovereign Pontiff alone who gathers all in his arms, not excepting tailors. Here, if they could but know it, is their blessed comfort! ... Postscript: I am persuaded of this; that it is utterly impossible for a man to be a *true gentleman* who is not of the true Church. ... Whatever Evan may think of himself, or Rose think of him, I *know the thing.*" This scathing exposure of sentimentalism in its religious, or rather pseudo-religious phase, echoes the third last paragraph of "Vanity Fair," though Becky evidently did not "know the thing."

Her mother's unflinching sincerity* and Lady Jocelyn's transparent magnanimity are an adequate foil to Louisa's trickery. Of the minor characters, Jack Raikes has a rôle similar to that of Braintop in "Sandra Belloni," but he might have been the brother of Dick Swiveller; in him as in the eccentric brothers Cogglesby, Meredith has indulged in a broad humour which becomes riotous farce, and

* The picnic-scene (ch. xxx—xxxi) is parallel to the similar episode in "Sandra Belloni" (ch. xxxi—xxxii), when Mrs. Chump appears at the fête.

George Meredith

this is barely tempered by the pathetic, morbid little figure of Juliana Bonner. Her fate resembles that of Clare Doria Forey in the preceding novel,* but she is spiteful in her relations to Rose, as Clare never could have been.

The most notable passages in the novel, so far as description goes, are the fantastic digression upon habits (ch. viii), the opening of ch. x, the wine-chapter (ch. xii),† the cricket-match (ch. xiii), the love-scene between Rose and Evan beside the stream (ch. xxiii), and the various inn-episodes at the Green Dragon, the Aurora, and the Dolphin.

The Spanish story, to which the Duke alludes in ch. xxii, is told of Villamediana (1582 —1622), who, during a fire which took place at the performance of one of his masques in 1622, gallantly carried out Queen Isabel de Bourbon. The Queen had been acting in the play. For this and other indiscretions the cavalier had to pay with his life.

---

* There is another minor parallel. One touch of nature makes the sexes kin. Lady Jocelyn (in ch. xvii), notes that the Countess is a female euphuist in her talk. " She has made a capital selection of her vocabulary from Johnson." Berry, Sir Austin Feverel's valet, also uses dictionary words, which he collects from a pocket-Johnson.

† " Both Ale and Eve seem to speak imperiously to the soul of man. See that they be good, see that they come in season, and we bow to the consequences."

SANDRA BELLONI

Sandra Belloni

THIS novel, which originally appeared in 1864 under the title of "Emilia in England," is the only story which Meredith furnished with a sequel. After publishing "Evan Harrington," he wrote nothing but poetry for three years, and then published three novels in three years, "Rhoda Fleming" intervening between the two "Emilia" books. Both of the latter throb with that keen sympathy for the Italians in their struggle for liberty which Meredith had already voiced incidentally in "The Ordeal of Richard Feverel," where Richard and Lady Judith Felle sighed sentimentally over the plight of Italy. "Who has not wept for Italy? I see the aspirations of a world arise for her, thick and frequent as the puffs of smoke from cigars of Pannonian sentries." Emilia's passion for Italy is the central theme of "Sandra Belloni" as well as of its sequel. "Whenever I think of Italy,

139

night or day, pant-pant goes my heart. The name of Italy is my nightingale : I feel that somebody lives that I love, and is ill-treated shamefully, crying out to me for help." The very phrases about Emilia run into poetry. Her wonderful figure dominates this novel, even when she is off the scene, and the variety of comedy, burlesque, pathos, and even tragedy which Meredith has crowded into its pages runs up in the end into the single impression of the heroine's personality. She represents the artistic temperament combined with a soul, with a deep passion for her country and with the power of inspiring and enjoying human affections. James Thomson declared, "For integral grandeur and originality of conception, and for perfectness of execution, the heroine of his "Emilia" appears to me the sovereign character of our modern fiction." This is too largely said. Even if the range of comparison is narrowed to Meredith's own fiction, Diana would dispute the primacy of Emilia.* Into both women Meredith has

---

* Both can be impulsive and at the same time are capable of aplomb and coolness. Powys told Emilia that she should never act from an impulse which was not the impulse of all her nature. She needed the advice, and Meredith constantly shows how his best women-characters take long to decide on a course of importance.

Sandra Belloni

put a great deal of his own heart and soul, and many—perhaps from insular prejudice—will prefer the Irish beauty to the Italian, the novelist to the singer. Thomson carries us with him, however, in the comment on Meredith's style which he published in his "Note on George Meredith" (1876), reprinted in his "Essays and Phantasies," a comment which applies pre-eminently to this novel and its predecessor. "His style is very various and flexible, flowing freely in whatever measures the subject and the mood may dictate. At its best it is so beautiful in simplest Saxon, so majestic in rhythm, so noble with noble imagery, so pregnant with meaning, so vital and intense, that it must be ranked among the supreme achievements of our literature."

The outline of the story is as follows :

Emilia Alessandra Belloni is the daughter of Guiseppe Belloni, an Italian revolutionary; her English* mother had married him after he had been obliged to fly as an exile to

---

* Partly Welsh, it appears. This is one of the traits which afterwards drew her to Merthyr Powys and Georgiana. "All subtle feelings are discerned by Welsh eyes when untroubled by any mental agitation. Brother and sister were Welsh, and I may observe that there is human nature and Welsh nature " (ch. xxviii).

141

George Meredith

London.* He is a violinist in the orchestra of the Italian Opera, but becomes a drunken wretch, who wishes to make capital dishonourably out of his daughter's musical talent. She escapes from him into the country, where her singing is overheard by the daughters and the partner of Mr. Pole, a wealthy London merchant, whose estate is in the neighbourhood. The daughters simply wish to exploit her music in order to advance their own social ambitions, but Mr. Pericles, their father's partner, has higher aims for her. Antonio Pericles Agriopoulos is a Greek who has an overpowering passion for music; he "held millions of money as dust compared to a human voice," and, in his rapture over Emilia's singing, he proposes to dominate her career. He will train her to be a queen of opera. "Yeaz! I am made my mind! I send her abroad to ze Académie for one, two, tree year. She shall be instructed as was not before. Zen a noise at La Scala. No—Paris! No—London! She shall astonish London fairst.—Yez! if I take a theatre! Yez! if I buy a newspaper! Yez!

* His experience resembled that described by Browning in "The Italian in England."

Sandra Belloni

if I pay feefty-sossand pound!" He gets her
father's consent to take her to Italy. But,
unluckily for the connoisseur's programme,
Emilia loses her heart to Wilfrid Pole, a
young soldier, who loves his sister's protegée
in a gallant, sentimental fashion. His own
prospects, however, and a sense of duty to
his father, oblige him at the same time to entangle himself with Lady Charlotte Chilling-
worth,* with whom he has been philandering.
Emilia, who has given up Italy for his sake,
is at first incredulous; her trustful nature is
shocked by the revelation of her lover's duplicity, which for a long while she refuses to
credit. Her appeal to Mr. Pole drives the
merchant into a fit; his affairs make it necessary that Lady Charlotte should be Wilfrid's
wife. Emilia meantime is rescued from her
father, who is acting in the interests of

* Lady Charlotte at first seems to belong to the class of the de Courcys
whom Trollope delighted to pourtray, but Meredith develops her character
with some subtlety. Wilfrid, he says, was not in love with her; he was
simply in harness to her, feeling that her strength of character brought out
something in himself. She saw his faults but liked him none the less that
she felt she could help him and be a mate for him. What disgusted her was
his double-dealing. She was too generous to be jealous of Emilia, even
when the latter fascinated Wilfrid away from her. "Being of a nature
leaning to great-mindedness, though not of the first rank, she could not
meanly mask her own deficiency by despising it. To do this is the secret
evil by which souls of men and women stop their growth."

George Meredith

Pericles, and Lady Charlotte, in order to spare her feelings and to cure her of her infatuation for the youth, arranges for her to overhear Wilfrid's declaration to herself at an inn in Dover. The poor girl, on being convinced of his treachery, collapses under the shock, and flies to London, where she nurses her despair under the protection of an Italian patriot, Marini, and his wife, who had already rescued her from the machinations of her father. She clings to the consolation that if she has lost her lover, she still has her voice. The proposal of Pericles now appears to be her one chance of happiness; she goes to his office and offers to accept his programme. But the strain of the past few months and a severe cold have temporarily affected her throat. Pericles, who has followed Belloni in a wild-goose chase after Emilia, is naturally exasperated at her silly philandering with Wilfrid as well as at her misuse of her voice; he rudely dismisses her, with the threat that he will put her father on her track. "You shall go to old Belloni; and, crack, if ze voice will come back to a whip,—bravo, old Belloni!" Terrified at the thought of falling

Sandra Belloni

once more into her father's clutches, Emilia tries to hide herself in London. She is eventually rescued by Merthyr Powys, a Welsh squire who loves Italy; he has befriended her from the first with a loyal, unselfish affection, and now carries her off to stay with his half-sister,* where she may regain her health and self-confidence before travelling with them to begin her studies in Italy.

Emilia, however, is destined to reach Italy in another way. She learns accidentally that Wilfrid proposes to enter the Austrian army, where his uncle is a general. This news hurts her far more than the prospect of his marriage to Lady Charlotte. She cannot bear to think of him serving against her beloved Italy, and, in a paroxysm of patriotic emotion, she promises Wilfrid that she will stay in England if he refuses to wear the Austrian white coat. Wilfrid, who has been hanging about her for months, takes advantage of her promise and agrees to the stipulation; as Powys has left for Italy, he thinks the coast is now clear for a resump-

---

* Georgiana Ford is a sterling woman, who is great enough to overcome her jealousy of Emilia and her dislike of Italian revolutions, out of sheer loyalty to Merthyr.

tion of his own courtship. Emilia soon feels the bondage of her impulse and hasty promise. The folly of it dawns on her, when she realises that her heart is in Italy, where an uprising of the patriots has taken place; but she is chained by her word, and Wilfrid selfishly refuses to release her. At last she summons up courage to break her promise. Before she leaves England, however, she is able to come to the aid of Mr. Pole and his family, who are in danger of being ruined by Pericles. Mr. Pole, in order to marry off his children grandly and to maintain the extravagant household on which his daughters insist, has been tempted to speculate and to misappropriate trust-funds belonging to a vulgar, Irish widow, Mrs. Chump. Pericles, exasperated at the Poles, and especially Wilfrid, for having ruined Emilia's career, refuses to pay up what his partner owes. At this crisis, Emilia's voice returns to her; she arranges for Pericles to overhear her,* and the Greek, overjoyed at the prospect of saving her for her true

* This scene, entitled "Frost on a May Night" (ch. lviii), recalls not only the opening episode of the novel, but the poem entitled "A Night of Frost in May," where, as in "Farina," Meredith describes in inimitable words the singing of the nightingales.

Sandra Belloni

vocation, promises to settle Mr. Pole's affairs, provided that Emilia will accompany her mother to the Milan Conservatorio and for three years put her art above politics and love-making.* Emilia thus leaves for Italy under the auspices of Pericles, not of Powys.

The closing episode of the novel enables Meredith to administer his final blow to the vanity of the Misses Pole. These superfine ladies, who affected to despise Emilia and who patronised her simply for the sake of the social credit they hoped to win from her, live to see their pride and sentimentalism shattered, and are forced to accept deliverance from ruin at the hand of this unselfish and forgiving little lady. "Sandra Belloni" is Meredith's full-length study of sentimentalism, in its tragic as well as its comic aspects. He scourges the social pretensions of the parvenus, indeed; but this is done elsewhere in the novels, and the group of the Misses Pole, especially Cornelia, is selected as typical of

* "It is a little grief to me that I think this man loves music more deeply than I do." This confession, made in her letter to Powys (ch. lix), will be better understood when "Vittoria" is read. The letter itself, with its outpouring of frank and shy affection, makes it more difficult than ever to understand how the writer of it could treat Powys as she did afterwards in Italy; in this respect she falls below the level of Diana and Carinthia.

George Meredith

the feminine sentimentalist in full blossom, who finds herself in the end the prey of un-realities, and entangled in hypocrisies, deceits, and suffering. Meredith suggests that they inherited this tendency. Their father, he remarks, "was one of those men who have no mental, little moral, feeling. With him feeling was almost entirely physical, as it was intensely so. That is the key to Mr. Pole, and to not a few besides. It is certainly a degree in advance of no feeling at all, and may give to many people who are never tried, the reputation of good parents, jolly friends, ex-cellent citizens."* Mr. Pole and his family, however, had the misfortune to be tried.

Like the three daughters of the great Mel, the Misses Pole have a brother. Wilfrid is depicted as the youthful sentimentalist in love, an egoist of Sir Willoughby Patterne's type upon the minor scale, and Meredith has etched him to the very quick. Like Evan, he is in the unformed period of life,

* "He was neat, insignificant, and nervously cheerful; with the eyes of a bird, that let you into no interior" (ch. xiv). Andrew Cogglesby was another kind of bird: "he eyed every man living with the benevolence of a patriarch, dashed with the impudence of a London sparrow" ("Evan Harrington," ch. viii).

but the tailor comes out of it better than the cornet; while Evan rises to the occasion, Wilfrid proves too much of a sentimentalist to retain any deep impressions. He liked to be comfortable and to feel himself important, either as Lady Charlotte's husband or as the champion of Emilia. He was not so much a coxcomb, says Meredith, as a man who was desperately afraid of ridicule and fond of sentiment; his gallantry and courage were handicapped by these weaknesses, and he was very properly jilted by both the women with whom he trifled. In ch. liii a farcical application of this anti-sentimental philosophy is thrown out, by way of interlude, but Meredith elsewhere analyses it with some seriousness. The false and fantastic passion of sentiment he calls "riding on the Hippogriff" (see chapters xliv and li). Real passion is "noble strength on fire," and it never makes its possessor unnatural or artificial. It "may tug against commonsense but is never, in a great nature, divorced from it." The sentimentalist, on the contrary, unconsciously loves feeling for feeling's sake; he becomes high-flying and absurd in his demands to have it gratified;

149

what excites him is not the object itself so much as the emotions which it is able to excite in him, and this morbid craving prevents him from realizing his proper condition as well as from appreciating the profound passion which lifts and sustains human nature in the pursuit of a worthy object. The spurious passion of the sentimentalist confines him to the circle of his own emotions. It renders him irritable, short-sighted, and essentially selfish.

The forty-fourth chapter also reveals another vein of Meredith's mind. German sentimentalism, as Richter wittily observed, inculcated "a universal love for all men and all beasts — except reviewers." Meredith loathed sentimentalism but he was at one with it in making this exception, and "Sandra Belloni" contains the first of the sarcastic, almost bitter, comments upon English reviewers (as well as upon the English public) which spurt up throughout the later novels, whenever the author feels obliged to defend his own psychological method (see above p. 114). In his review of "Owen Meredith's" poetical effusions, four years later, he wrote : "Reviewers of poetry are always able men—able

Sandra Belloni

to express their opinions—and between heavy
puffs and contemptuous notices, the public
gains from them in the end some approximate
idea of a poet's value." This is less truculent
than the paragraph in ch. xliii of "Sandra
Belloni"; but he did not always rein in his
scorn for reviewers of fiction so successfully.*
Tracy Runningbrook, in this novel, is, like
Agostino and even Lydiard afterwards, a finer
plant than Diaper Sandoe in "The Ordeal of
Richard Feverel," but he is less attractive
than the young Arthur Rhodes whom Diana
generously championed. There is more about
music than about poetry, however, from the
passage on the drum (ch. ix) to the eulogy of
Beethoven and the description of Emilia playing on the harp in the booth (ch. xi). The
operatic stars appear in ch. xxxii as they do
later in "One of Our Conquerors" (ch. xx).
Sir Purcell is an organist but it was not till
the twelfth chapter of "Beauchamp's Career"
that Meredith elaborated his philosophy of
the organ as a symbol of monarchism. The

* Art-critics get their passing flick of the whip in the fifth chapter of
"One of Our Conquerors." They are "sometimes unanimous, and are
then taken for guides, and are fatal."

George Meredith

zither is described in the twenty - seventh chapter of "Vittoria," and in the forty-fifth chapter of that novel the effect of the military drum is analysed.

In Mrs. Chump, the stout, coarse, good-hearted Irish widow, Meredith has given play to the element of farce which he had indulged with such riotous effects in "Evan Harrington." Mrs. Chump is drawn in broad caricature; her blue satin, her brogue, her love of liquor, her ill-concealed affection for poor Mr. Pole, and her distressing frankness of speech, all drive the ladies of Brookfield out of "fine shades and nice feelings" into an inferno of torture. Mrs. Chump does not see why she should not become the second Mrs. Pole, and her suspicions of Mr. Pole's honesty give her a hold upon that distracted gentleman which makes her, as well as Emilia, an instrument of retribution upon the ladies who had formerly scorned and insulted her. The scenes at the supper (ch. xxxii) and with Braintop (ch. xxxv)* show her at her richest;

* The theatre-scene (ch. xxv), where the amorous clerk gazes up at Emilia, is oddly reminiscent of the similar scene in "Bleak House" (ch. xiii). But Mr. Guppy was not so careful of his locks and general appearance as Braintop was.

but she is always vital, and her naturalness
forms a foil to the silly affectation and artificiality of the Misses Pole,* just as the sterling
chivalry of Merthyr Powys and even the
artistic enthusiasm of Pericles are meant to
throw Wilfrid's shallowness into sharp relief.

The suicide of Sir Purcell Barrett, Cornelia's
rejected lover, comes with an unexpected
shock, but Meredith evidently intended from
the first to strike this sterner note.   Pride and
sentimentalism are an opening for more than
laughter, he insists ; they may lead to tragedy
as well as to social complications.   The yacht-
episode, on the other hand, is out of proportion,
and the description of Mr. Pole's illness leans
to the long side, but the country-house scenes
are as rich as in " Evan Harrington," and the
fencing between the Tinleys and the Poles
shows Mr. Meredith's dramatic power at its
very best upon the petty scale.   The beer-
chapters (viii, ix, and xi) recall the eighth poem
of "Modern Love," which had been pub-

---

* " Why," Mrs. Chump expostulates, " if they was to be married at the
altar, they'd stare and be 'ffendud if ye asked them if they was thinking
of their husbands, they would ! ' Oh, dear, no ! and ye' re mistaken, and
we 're thinkin' o' the coal-scuttle in the back parlour,'—or somethin' about
souls, if not coals."

George Meredith

lished two years earlier, and the twentieth
poem of that series ("That man I do suspect
A coward who would burden the poor deuce
With what ensues from his own slipperiness")
anticipates the analysis of Sir Purcell in the
beginning of ch. lv. The absurdity of reproaching Providence for our mishaps had
been already noticed in "Evan Harrington"
(ch. x), however, and Meredith stops to under-
line it more than once in the later novels, just
as the passage on adversity in ch. xviii ("This
fellow had been fattening all his life on pros-
perity ; the very best dish in the world : but
it does not prove us," etc.) is a prose variation
on the theme of "Hard Weather" and "The
Empty Purse" ("A Conservative youth ! who
the cream-bowl skimmed, Desiring affairs to
be left as they are," etc.)

RHODA FLEMING

Rhoda Fleming.

IN "Rhoda Fleming," published the year
after "Emilia in England," Meredith
essayed the delicate and difficult task of describing the innate purity of a woman after a
moral lapse. The story is superior in grasp
and strength to Mrs. Gaskell's "Ruth";
the difference of scale makes it less easy
to compare it with "Adam Bede," but the
outstanding feature of its treatment is the
prominence assigned to the punishment
not of the woman so much as of the man.
Unlike his own "enamoured sage,"Meredith
never passes his honest readers "through the

---

* Compare "Odes in Contribution to the Song of French History"
(1898), page 58, with their description of France in 1870 :—

> "She sees what seed long sown, ripened of late,
> Bears this fierce crop ; and she discerns her fate
> From origin to agony, and on
> As far as the wave washes long and wan
> Off one disastrous impulse : for of waves
> Our life is, and our deeds are pregnant graves
> Blown rolling to the sunset from the dawn."

George Meredith

sermon's dull defile," but this poignant tale*
reads like a lay-sermon on the text: "Be not
deceived; God is not mocked; for what a
man soweth, that shall he also reap." Edward
Blancove has a remorse like that of Lovelace
in Richardson's great novel, but his punishment resembles that meted out to Lord
Fleetwood in "The Amazing Marriage";
both repent too late.

Dahlia and Rhoda Fleming are the daughters, fair and dark, of a Kentish yeoman-
farmer. Their story is a study in the development of country-girls who have innocent social
ambitions or aspirations, and who start with
sentimental ideas about London and London-
life. For them "the mysterious metropolis
flew with fiery fringes through dark space, in
their dreams." * This romantic prepossession
inclines them for any move which promises
to gratify their social desires to rise. An
avenue is soon opened to them. After their
mother's death, her brother Anthony
Hackbut appears on the scene. An old money
porter at Boyne's Bank in London, he has the

* Contrast the vehement description of London simultaneously published
by Ruskin in the " Crown of Wild Olive."

reputation at Queen Anne's Farm of being rich and miserly—a reputation which he secretly enjoys. Dahlia goes up to keep house for him, and happens, as she accompanies him to the bank, to meet a young lawyer of 23 years of age, Edward Blancove, the son of Sir William Blancove, at present head of the bank. His admiration for her fresh country beauty is undisguised. The casual acquaintance ripens into something warmer. The lovers meet secretly, and Dahlia's education is advanced, at Edward's orders, by attendance at various classes.

Presently, feeling neglected by his niece, Anthony goes down again to Queen Anne's Farm, to bring up Rhoda. Like her sister, she has the provincial's idealization of the metropolis. "Great powerful London—the new universe to her spirit—was opening its arms to her." She happens to arrive on the very night when Edward had succeeded in persuading Dahlia to elope ; the latter, returning to Anthony's lodgings for her mother's Bible, is surprised to find Rhoda sleeping in her bed, and is pulled up in time. But only for a time. Rhoda returns, after her London visit, to the

George Meredith

Farm, and the next news is a letter from Dahlia who, as "Mrs Edward Ayrton," has eloped to the Continent with her lover. The farmer's suspicions of his daughter are aroused, though Rhoda's loyal heart still fights down its uneasiness.

Meantime Rhoda is mildly pursued by young Algernon Blancove, a clerk at Boyne's Bank, who had chanced to see her there, as his cousin Edward had seen her sister. Algernon, the son of Squire Blancove, whose property adjoins Queen Anne's Farm, is a weak fashionable youth, whose philandering is easily frustrated by Robert Armstrong, the farmer's assistant, himself in love with Rhoda. His real name is Robert Eccles. The son of a Hampshire yeoman-farmer, he had enlisted, after a wild time in youth, in a cavalry regiment where Algernon had chanced to be an officer. Out of this, thanks to a small legacy, he was able to buy himself. Taking to farming, and changing his name, he had been able to curb his passions, thanks to Rhoda's influence, and now he endeavours to keep her from Algernon, whom he knows to be a mixture of the fool and the rascal.

Rhoda Fleming

On Dahlia's return to London, her father and Rhoda go up to see her, but the girl is ashamed to face them. Her lover pleads for the delay of their marriage, on account of his prospects. He conceals the liaison from his own family, and she sadly agrees to avoid her relatives. The crisis comes when, in a London theatre, the farmer and Rhoda chance to recognise Dahlia in the company— not of Edward, who meanly remains in the background—but of Algernon who is employed by his cousin to get the girl out of the theatre, unknown to her relatives. This accident naturally throws the Flemings on to a false scent. Algernon is deemed the culprit, and Dahlia is disowned by her crushed, indignant, unforgiving father. Rhoda alone champions her sister, whilst Robert, though refusing to share her faith, undertakes to tackle the supposed villain Algernon, whom he now suspects of designs upon Rhoda as well. He tracks the youth to a country-house in Hampshire, where the house-party includes both Edward and Algernon. The former has begun to repent of his escapade and to seek relief from his connexion with Dahlia.

"Already he looked back upon Dahlia from a prodigious distance. He knew that there was something to be smoothed over; something written in the book of facts which had to be smeared out, and he seemed to do it, while he drank the bubbling wine and heard himself talk. . . . He closed, as it were, a black volume, and opened a new and bright one. Young men easily fancy that they may do this, and that, when the black volume is shut, the tide is stopped. Saying "I was a fool," they believe they have put an end to the foolishness. What father teaches them that a human act once set in motion flows on for ever to the great account?" Edward's mood of disgust is fostered by the cynical worldliness of the seniors with whom he mixes, and also by the luxury of his present surroundings. In addition to this he is feeling anew the fascination of his lovely cousin and hostess, Mrs. Margaret Lovell, a blonde young widow, whose "beauty shone as from an illumination of black flame, under the light of two duels" fought about her in India. It is at this moment that Robert's pursuit of Algernon irritates Edward. Farmer Eccles' farm, at Warbeach village, adjoins the country-house, and Robert, determined to find out what Algernon (the supposed seducer) has done with Dahlia, attacks the youth twice at the hunt, and is only pacified by the adroitness of Mrs. Lovell, who undertakes to satisfy the irate champion of Dahlia. Meanwhile, maddened by this interference, Edward, who has allowed Algernon to borrow his name in order to ward off persecution, pays money to Nic Sedgett, an old enemy of Robert, to make a murderous attack on him, whilst Mrs. Lovell fools him on the next day by her wit and charms. Robert then discovers that he has mistaken Algernon for Edward, and scorning to touch Nic Sedgett,* threatens and challenges the young lawyer. The latter now finds himself in a coil of awkward consequences. But he is too vain to admit his

---

* "Leave real rascals to the Lord above," he tells his friend and landlady, Mrs. Boulby. "He's safe to punish them. They've stepped outside the chances. That's my idea. I wouldn't go out of my way to kick them—not I! It's the half-and-half villains we've got to dispose of. They're the mischief." Nic Sedgett is Meredith's nearest approach to a villain. Yet even he is not a villain in the true sense of the term. The hero and villain of the tale are, as Meredith points out, combined in Edward. Selfish and cunning, Sedgett has no deep-laid plot of his own. The initiative does not rest with him. He is rather the tool of others, acting in accordance with his low nature upon their suggestion, and carrying out their plans.

cowardice and act justly towards his victim, and so has recourse to subterfuges. He pretends to suppose that Dahlia, whose only reproach to him was her suffering, participated in the scheme to worry him; snatching at this miserable pretext for blaming her, he disappears to Paris, leaving the matter in the hands of Mrs. Lovell. Her plan is to make provision (including a husband) for Dahlia, as the easiest way of ending the entanglement. Consequently she still endeavours to keep Robert in ignorance of Dahlia's whereabouts, but is brought to terms by the appearance on the scene of Major Percy Waring, a friend and former fellow officer of Robert, whose previous acquaintance with the fair widow enables him to force her hand. By this time, however, Dahlia is invisible. Deserted by her lover, she has had brain-fever, and has fallen in accidentally with Nic Sedgett, who has shown some kindness to her. He had undertaken, for a large sum of money, to marry the girl and then emigrate. The pivot of the whole story lies in Dahlia's reasons for agreeing to this extraordinary step, and in the ways, partly deliberate, partly accidental, by which

Rhoda Fleming

it is executed. Dahlia's illness has sapped
her spirit. Though still in love with Edward,
she brings herself to marry Sedgett simply
for the sake of protection. Marriage, she felt,
would secure her good name, wipe the spot
of shame from her character, and enable her
to face her father and sister again. Hence
she could rise, trembling and bewildered, to
sacrifice her happiness and love, for the sake
of being made an "honest woman" in her
relatives' eyes. In this resolve she is stoutly
abetted, even urged, by Rhoda, who overbears
any hesitation on the part of her shrinking
sister. Even Robert favours the step ; for,
ignorant who the proposed husband is, he
feels Dahlia's marriage is the one means of
restoring her to her family and thus securing
her own happiness. The catastrophe is
furthered, also, by the foolish blundering of
Algernon, who does not forward Dahlia's
pathetic letters of appeal to Edward, and
spends on himself the money sent by his
cousin to buy off Sedgett. For meanwhile
Edward has been coming to his right mind.
His flight to Paris, "leaving all the brutality
to be done for him behind his back," had put

George Meredith

a chasm between him and Mrs. Lovell. The latter, now under the better guidance of Major Waring, visits Dahlia and honestly seeks to provide for her future by means of this marriage. At the same time she throws over Edward, who, still forced to believe that Dahlia is agreeable to the marriage, and perhaps * ignorant as yet that the husband is Sedgett, is roused from his cynicism and inaction by receiving at last poor Dahlia's letters. He hurries home to stop the marriage and avow his connexion with Dahlia. But the repentance is too late. Partly owing to Algernon's folly in refusing to carry out his telegraphed directions, partly as a result of Dahlia's passive weakness, but chiefly owing to Rhoda's not unnatural suspicion of her sister's seducer and her resolute determination to make the frail girl reach the altar, Edward's frantic efforts to get an interview with his mistress (and so avert the marriage) are in vain, though seconded at the end by Robert, who

* " It may not, perhaps, be said that he had distinctly known Sedgett to be the man. He had certainly suspected the possibility of his being the man. It is out of the power of most wilful and selfish natures to imagine, so as to see accurately, the deeds they prompt or permit to be done. They do not comprehend them until these black realities stand up before their eyes." **Ch. xxxvii (end)**.

166

Rhoda Fleming

begins dimly to suspect that something **is** wrong. After the ceremony Sedgett brutally flings Dahlia off. She returns, however, in peace to the farm and her father. But a delayed letter from Edward reveals to her the terrible mistake she has just committed, and her frenzied anguish stirs compunction in poor Rhoda's heart for the sorrow which she has caused by doing what she had believed was for the best. Robert and she now undertake the defence of Dahlia from Sedgett. When the latter appears to claim his wife with coarse brutality, he is supported by the farmer who is unable to comprehend why a husband's rights should not be upheld. Dahlia, in her extremity, attempts to poison herself. But, in the nick of time, it is discovered that the marriage is invalid. Sedgett, it turns out, had been playing a double game. Already married, he had agreed to marry Dahlia simply for the sum of money offered by the Blancoves. Dahlia consequently is free. She recovers from her poison, but her life is shattered. The rose of womanhood has become a frail bent lily, and Edward's penitence fails to requicken her affections.

167

"She would marry him," Mrs. Lovell explains, "if she could bring herself to it;— the truth is, he killed her pride. Her taste for life is gone." Rhoda marries Robert, and Mrs. Lovell, ruined by her mania for betting, deserts Major Waring for the rich Sir William Blancove. Thus Edward missed both the women of his desire, the society dame as well as the country-girl. Through his cowardice he had forfeited his fair cousin's esteem, whilst the victory over his pride came too late to preserve for him the love of the rustic beauty with whom he had trifled.

The convivial scene, without which no novel of Meredith would be quite complete, occurs in chapter xviii. One of his keenest analyses of the French character is put into chapter xxii, and chapter xxvii opens with a handful of sentences which are quite in the vein of Carlyle. The forty-third chapter contains a well-known example of Meredithian dialogue, fortunately with a key supplied in brackets, but the novel as a whole is remarkably free from Meredithese; it is rare to meet with such lapses as "vulnerability" in the mouth of a yeoman (chapter xxiv).

Rhoda Fleming

The two weak points in the construction of the story are Dahlia's consent to marry Sedgett and the rôle of Mrs. Lovell. The latter, an Anglo-Indian "Venus Annodomini" after Mr. Kipling's heart, has a part too important for her character. "A far-fetched motive, an ingenious evasion of the issue, a witty instead of a passionate turn, offend us like an insincerity," says Stevenson. "All should be plain, all straightforward to the end. Hence it is that, in 'Rhoda Fleming,' Mrs. Lovell raises such resentment in the reader; her motives are too flimsy, her ways are too equivocal, for the weight and strength of her surroundings." Much more satisfactory is the treatment of pride in the various characters, particularly in Anthony Hackbut and in Edward. The former has the vanity of riches, or rather of the reputation for riches; money acts on his imagination and fires his brain (compare chapter xxv); he risks his good character in order to live up to the false character which he has taught his poorer relatives to attribute to him (compare chapter xl). Edward's pride is much more tragic and subtle. His pride of position keeps him from

169

avowing his relationship with Dahlia ; later on, his false pride leads him to subterfuges which force him into cowardice and selfishness ; and finally, when this meaner pride is killed by the crisis, it is too late.

VITTORIA

Vittoria

THIS sequel to "Sandra Belloni" appeared in the "Fortnightly Review" for 1866, the year* when Meredith was acting as war-correspondent for the "Morning Post" in Italy and Austria. It narrates the experiences of Emilia in Italy during 1848-1849. There the revolution broke out on January 2nd, 1848, at Milan, and then at Venice; the temporary success of the insurgents ended on the 23rd of March, 1849, at the battle of Novara, which led to the abdication of Charles Albert, and the historical scene of action in "Vittoria" practically lies between these two dates.† The novel contains a series of vivid military

---

* Ibsen settled in Rome in the autumn of 1866. But how differently he and Meredith viewed Italy!

† "Vittoria" is Meredith's contribution to the volume of generous sympathy with the Italian struggle for freedom, which threw up such remarkable waves in the English poetry and prose of last century. He does not write as a partisan, but his account of Italy's plight answers to that of Fogazzaro in "Piccolo Mondo antico."

scenes, plots, and intrigues, but these have spoiled the symmetry of the story. The thread of Vittoria's personality, which constitutes the real unity of its chapters, disappears altogether, now and then; episodes are heaped on episodes; Austrians, Italians, and English folk crowd the pages with more or less irrelevance; and, although Meredith pleads that "these half-comic little people have their place in the history of higher natures and darker destinies," his method assigns some of them more than their due stroke in the plot. This applies particularly to the English characters retained from "Sandra Belloni." The foreigners are more vital, but there are too many of them, and their under-plots and counter-plots form a whirling kaleidoscope, in which it is often difficult to keep the central figures in sight.

The novel follows this scheme of events :—

Emilia, on leaving England, had changed her name to Vittoria Campa ("her own name being an attraction to the blow-flies in her own country"). In terms of her agreement with Pericles, she had studied for three years at the Milan Conservatorio, and abstained from any

political action. But while her voice had
developed, her passion for Italy had also
grown deeper with the years, and it is arranged
that she is to make her début as a prima donna
at La Scala, in an opera written for the purpose
by one of the patriots, which, at one point, is
to give the signal for the Milanese rising
against the Austrians.

The novel opens on the eve of this début.
Mazzini, who is at the head of the plot, trusts
and admires Vittoria, but several of the conspirators have only too good reason to suspect
women, and especially singers. They dislike
the idea of Vittoria's co-operation, and
unluckily she gives them some apparent cause
to doubt her, by entering into correspondence
with her old friends Adela Pole (now Mrs
Sedley), and Wilfrid Pole (now Lieutenant
Pierson, serving with his uncle in the Austrian
army). Her letters are innocent but indiscreet.
They force Barto Rizzo, the agent of Count
Medole, an aristocratic leader of the conspir-
acy, to conclude that Vittoria must be either
an idiot or a traitor; in either case she is unfit
to be trusted with so important a part in the
plot. Barto is a study in the headstrong,

suspicious conspirator, whose error lies in his conceit and in his doubts of women. Imagining that he knows what should be done, better even than Mazzini, he determines, in the temporary absence of the chief, to have the rising postponed. Vittoria is equally determined to go on with her opera, however; she hotly resents the suspicions of her loyalty. Pericles attempts to kidnap her with the aid of Captain Weisspriess, an Austrian officer; he hopes to tame her into a state where she will be kindled by the passion of love, not of politics, and, like Carlo Ammiani, who is in love with her, he foresees the risk of letting her sing, as had been arranged, at La Scala on the appointed evening. But, by the cleverness of Beppo, one of Vittoria's bodyguard, the plot fails; her rival, Irma di Karski, is kidnapped in her stead, and Vittoria does appear, to win an instant success by her magnificent singing, in the patriotic opera. "The house rose, Italians and Germans together. Genius, music, and enthusiasm break the line of nationalities." Vittoria closes the opera by singing the unprinted lyric which had been agreed upon as the signal for the rising of

Vittoria

Young Italy, beginning :—
> "I cannot count the years,
>   That you will drink, like me,
>   The cup of blood and tears,
>   Ere she to you appears :—
>   *Italia, Italia, shall be free.*"

This defiance of the Austrians throws the audience into confusion. Pericles is in terror lest his precious singer should be injured by their knavish tricks and politics, but Vittoria is smuggled into safety by her well-wishers, and eventually ensconced, by the intervention of Weisspriess, at the Castle of Sonnenberg, near Meran. Meantime, Milan remains as before; no rising takes place; but Carlo Ammiani, the young Milanese conspirator who has aided his beloved to escape after the opera, is thrown into prison. Wilfrid joins the Lenkensteins* at Meran; he is engaged to Countess Lena, as he had been to Lady Charlotte in England, but he has fallen into disgrace with the Austrian authorities by helping Vittoria to escape from the theatre.

* Anna and Lena are described as the "German beauties of Milan, lively little women, and sweet." They become bitter enemies of Vittoria, particularly because she had helped Angelo Guidascarpi to escape, who had killed their brother Paul and wounded Weisspriess, Anna's lover.

George Meredith

Wilfrid's sentimentalism is not yet cured, and the least encouragement would attach him once more to Vittoria. She begins to feel the Austrian atmosphere of the Castle uncongenial and hostile, and uses Wilfrid to further some of her own plans. The party breaks up; Lena throws over Wilfrid; and Vittoria goes back to resume her professional career in Turin.

The autumn episodes of the story end here. With the twenty-ninth chapter Meredith begins the winter and spring episodes of the revolt and war in "the year of flames for continental Europe." Carlo, who escapes from prison, falls under the spell of the Countess Violetta d'Isorella, an aristocratic beauty of the royalist party, who, before her marriage, had stirred his boyish passions. Her characteristics are "a leaning towards evil, a light sense of shame, a desire for money, and in her heart a contempt for the principles she did not possess, but which, apart from the intervention of other influences, could occasionally sway her actions." She instils a doubt of Vittoria into his impressionable heart, and he, on starting for Brescia, sends a message to his mother that Vittoria must stay beside her at Milan. Violetta delivers the message to Vittoria in a careless way. Vittoria thinks it wiser to remain at Turin, where she is not only safe but able to make money on the stage for the patriotic cause. Carlo resents this disobedience. He cannot believe in Charles Albert,* "the wobbling king," as Vittoria does,† and, in a fit of ardent republicanism, he demands peremptorily that she shall leave Turin and break with her monarchical delusion. Thus the schism between monarchists and republicans which hurt the patriotic cause hurts the lovers also. Instead of obeying him, or of going to sing in London, as Pericles besought her, she considers it better to follow the king's army and help as far as she can in the liberation of Italy. Vittoria's mind is too independent to be swayed by Carlo at a distance. The latter

* Carlo shared the Mazzinist suspicions of Charles Albert, which, together with the king's military irresolution, helped to wreck the revolution.

† Compare Mrs Browning's tribute in "Casa Guidi Windows" (the second part). Meredith analyses Vittoria's view of the king into a sympathetic pity for one whom she thought misjudged. She prided herself on thinking "that she divined the king's character by mystical intuition." Slight touches of self-importance are also noted in chapters xxxi and xxxii.

George Meredith

fails to realise her strength of character, *
however, and he is wounded, alike in his
personal vanity and in his republican sympathies, by her repeated refusal to quit the
king.

Meantime, Pericles manages, with the aid of
the Austrians, to carry off his pearl of singers ;
Carlo rescues her, however, and she obeys
his injunction to join his mother at Brescia.
But instead of following the Countess to Lago
Maggiore, when the rebellion was collapsing
under Radetzsky's vigorous attack, Vittoria
stays on in Milan to nurse Merthyr Powys.
She is sincerely longing for her marriage with
Carlo, † yet the sight of Powys makes her feel
some compunction at the thought of leaving
him to recover from his wounds, only to find
her married. Carlo, in her absence, falls
once more under Violetta's spell; she advises

---

* "It is the curse of man's education in Italy. He can see that she
has wits and courage. He will not consent to make use of them. She,
who has both heart and judgment—she is merely a little boat tied to a big
ship." See "Sandra Belloni" (chap lii).

† Meredith (in ch. xxxv) admits her momentary lapse from devotion
to either music or patriotism. "She wept with longing for love and
dependence. She was sick of personal freedom. The blessedness of
marriage, of peace and dependence, came on her imagination like a soft
breeze from a hidden garden, like sleep."

him to postpone his marriage in the interests
of the cause, and when Vittoria rejoins his
mother and himself at Lago Maggiore, it is to
find the chill of silent blame resting on herself
for the delay in arriving. She finds a passion-
less courtesy in Carlo, who is more concerned
now for the cause in Lombardy than for
his marriage. Besides, his vanity has been
inflamed by Violetta ; Vittoria has wounded
his pride by her delay and disobedience ; and
finally he is told that Barto Rizzo's mad
suspicions would handicap his influence if
Vittoria were to take his name at the present
crisis. Eventually, however, Carlo's silly
pique is overcome, and the marriage takes
place. Merthyr Powys chivalrously exerts
his influence to bring it about, while Carlo
realises that Vittoria will need his name to
protect her against Rizzo's fanatical vengeance Their marriage serves to stir up the
enemies of Vittoria in Milan, including not
only the conspirators who blame her for
double-dealing, but also the women who envy
her beauty and voice. Vittoria is stabbed by
Rizzo's wife, but not fatally. Her suffering
makes Carlo remorseful for his past treat-

ment of her, before and after marriage, but he still ignores her wisdom and advice in his conceit of masculine superiority. "Her husband!" Pericles thunders, "oh! she must marry a young man, little donkey that she is! And he plays false to her. Good ; I do not object. But imagine in your own mind,—instead of passion, of rage, of tempest, she is frozen wiz a repose." Instead of pushing on to join Mazzini at Rome, as Vittoria and the rest urge, Carlo plots to make a fresh fight for Lombardy, where his plans have been already betrayed to the authorities by the heartless Violetta. His obstinate pride * refuses to listen to any remonstrances. Vittoria bewails her partial responsibility for his conduct.† "I could have turned my husband from this dark path ; I preferred to dream and sing. I would not see—it was my pride that would not see his error. My cowardice would not wound him with a single suggestion." In any

---

* Policy took the others to Rome ; Carlo said grandly that he would not leave beaten Lombardy, and admired himself, as he was admired by others, for this devotion. By the time that he saw through Violetta's treachery and his own folly, he had pledged himself to his followers too far to retreat. Read the penetrating paragraph at the opening of ch. xlv.

† The parallel between her and Nataly Radnor is very close at this point.

Vittoria

case, whether Carlo would have condescended
to listen to her or not, it is now too late to pull
him up. He heads the forlorn enterprise,
which is fore-doomed to failure. The battle
of Novara is fought, Brescia is bombarded,
and Carlo perishes with his party in their
flight. Vittoria's child is born safely, and
called Carlo Merthyr Ammiani. The reader
is left in the same tantalising uncertainty as at
the close of "Lord Ormont and his Aminta."
Did Vittoria ever change her last name to
Powys? It is to be hoped that she did.

"Like the swinging May-cloud that pelts
    the flowers with hailstones
Off a sunny border, she was made to
    bruise and bless."

She had bruised Powys often enough. He
deserved at least that she should bless him
even with a tardy gleam of sunshine.

Vittoria herself is the great figure in the
story. The superb creature dominates even
Pericles; she sways Mazzini to belief in her;
she catches the heart of the conspirators; she
impresses, even while she offends, the Italian
aristocrats with an inexplicable combination
of charm and resolution. Meredith praises

183

her singing enthusiastically. "Her voice
belonged to the order of the simply great
voices, and was a royal voice among them.
The great voice rarely astonishes our ears.
It illumines our souls." She puts her gift at
the service of the country, but her supreme
contribution to the struggle is the passionate
and tenacious idealism (see the passages in
chapters xv and xvi) of her faith in Italy.
This is one of the reasons why she and Carlo
disappoint one another ; he is the type of the
so-called practical conspirator, who is apt to
lose, in intrigues and compromises, the larger
vision to which Vittoria, like Mazzini, clung.

At the same time the total impression left
by Vittoria, it must be confessed, is somewhat
disappointing. She is a magnificent personality but she achieves little or nothing ; after
the great operatic scene, her influence is
scattered and fitful. She begins by behaving
with an indiscretion, almost amounting to
folly, in communicating with her old English
friends among the Austrians. Then she
repeats her English mistake by accepting the
love of Carlo ; he is at least a nobler character than Wilfrid, but he is no proper mate

184

Vittoria

for her, and it is only the glamour of his heady patriotism which blinds her to this ; her true mate, Merthyr Powys, is still passed over. The strain of the insurrection further weakens her into a mood of yearning for married bliss at one point, and into an almost flighty passion for the king at another. Thus, while it has become conventional to rank Vittoria as *prima inter pares* among the Meredithian heroines, a close analysis of the tale seems to show that, although her setting is heroic and her qualities those of a great soul, the author has not succeeded in conveying the impression of unity, intensity, and passionate absorption which we are entitled to expect from his delineation of the peerless singer into which the raw girl, Emilia, has developed.

But if Vittoria becomes in one sense less interesting than Emilia, Pericles waxes in force and favour. One's heart warms to this Greek millionaire. His divine passion for music has its humorous side, but there is something epic in his devotion to the art ; it is deeper than that of Vittoria herself. Vittoria is patriot, singer, and woman by turns. Pericles lives for music, or rather for the spiritual endowment of Vittoria's voice. He follows her anxiously even inside the fighting line. He threatens her, cajoles her, appeals to her, spends money for her, with the whole-hearted passion of the artistic nature which counts no sacrifice too great for its art. "I am possessed wiz passion for her voice. So it will be till I go to ashes. It is to me ze one zsing divine in a pig, a porpoise world." "Ser, if I wake not very late on Judgment-Day, I shall zen hear—but why should I talk poetry to you to make you laugh? I have a divin' passion for zat woman. Do I not give her to a husband, and say, Be happy! onnly sing! Be kissed! Be hugged! onnly give Pericles your voice." "It is not onnly voice he craves, but a soul, and Sandra, your countess, she has a soul." Meredith never again created the musical enthusiast with such power. The music-lovers in "One of Our Conquerors" are creeping things compared to this superb, vulgar, unselfish merchant, who is ready to spend his wealth for music and is wrathful because others will not see the duty of putting it before patriotism and love.

Vittoria

The course of the novel* is uninterrupted by the intrusion of the Philosopher's comments upon pride and sentimentalism which retard the progress of its lineal predecessor. In his humorous apology for the psychological digressions in "Sandra Belloni," Meredith announces that when Emilia is in Italy, the Philosopher proposes to keep entirely in the background, since in Italy "there is a field of action, of battles and conspiracies, nerve and muscle, where life fights for plain issues, and he can but sum results." We shall be quit of the Philosopher, my friends, "in the day when Italy reddens the sky with the banners of a land revived." This promise is kept. The defects of technique in "Vittoria" are not due to the love of abstract digressions, but to the fact that Meredith had several stories, instead of one, to tell, and that the exigencies of the historical background forced him to tell them all together, with the result that the masses of detail overlap, and a certain cumbrousness ensues. The supreme moments

* James Thomson applied to Meredith Coleridge's saying about Shakespeare, that "the intellectual power and the creative energy wrestle as in a war-embrace." In "Vittoria," which is crowded with phases of this combat, the creative energy is hardly ever overpowered in episodes.

or episodes are in the Mazzini-scenes at the beginning ("Vittoria" is one of the few novels in Meredith's list which open well); in the opera-chapters (ch. xviii—xxii); in ch. xxvi (the duel in the pass); and in the Rinaldo Guidascarpi passages. These do not win for "Vittoria" the position of primacy which is claimed among George Eliot's novels for "Romola"—written three years before. They do not even place "Vittoria" on a level with the older writer's Italian romance in point of symmetry and structure. But they introduce peasants, citizens, and soldiers who are not simply correct but vital; every figure in "Vittoria" throbs with reality, and the novel never leaves the impression of a manu-factured article which some of "Romola"'s more finished pages produce.

Like Carlyle's "French Revolution," the story requires to be read alongside of a plain historical summary of the period across which it throws quick flashes of light. Such a summary may be found by the English reader in the Countess Martinengo Cesaresco's "Liberation of Italy," in Mr. Bolton King's succinct "History of Italian Unity," or in

Vittoria

Mr. G. M. Trevelyan's fine historical study,
"Garibaldi's Defence of the Roman Repub-
lic." Mr. Trevelyan incidentally points out
that Laura Piaveni reproduces part of the
character of the Princess Belgiojoso, a high-
minded and devoted aristocratic adherent of
the revolution, while Luciano Romara is a
study of L. Manara, the Milanese aristocrat
who commanded the Lombard Bersaglieri
(see the allusion in ch. xii of "The Egoist").
The opening chapter of Carlyle's "Latter-day
Pamphlets" should also be read, in order to
catch the revolutionary throb of the period.

The Alpine scene at the opening is one of
the mountain-pictures which Meredith frequently painted (see below, under "The
Adventures of Harry Richmond"). Mazzini
himself, after crossing by the St. Gothard pass
to Milan in 1848, wrote: "no one knows
what poetry is, who has not found himself
there, at the highest point of the route, on the
plateau, surrounded by the peaks of the Alps
in the everlasting silence which speaks of
God. There is no atheism possible in the
Alps."

THE ADVENTURES
OF HARRY RICHMOND

The Adventures of Harry Richmond

THIS long novel, published in book form in 1871, is, like "The Ordeal of Richard Feverel," a study in the relations of father and son,* but it is written in the first person, and Harry plays a much less active rôle than Richard. When the story begins, Harry is carried off in his father's arms, and the hero, as boy or youth, has little initiative; he is always being carried on some tide, or swayed, to his good or undoing, by the influence of two or three stronger natures, particularly that of his father. Roy Richmond is the real hero of the story. Unlike Sir Austin, he wins the confidence of his boy, but his errors fail to wreck his son's happiness. Roy is a wonderful father. A preposterous adventurer, if you like, but not a scamp or scoundrel

---

* In both cases the father wrongs the son not by harshness but by misguided affection. Sir Austin's pride is in the system he has devised, Roy Richmond's in the ancestral dignity for which he conceives it his duty to train Harry. But while Harry's fortunes turn out happily, Richard's close in tragic gloom.

of the Barry Lyndon order. He is not even
bitten with the ambition of the great Mel ; his
social aspiration, for all its folly, is unselfishly
directed to what he conceives to be the best
interests of his boy ; if it is egoism, it is egoism
of the higher kind. The fascination of the
man, with his incorrigibly dramatic vein and
florid temper, throws Harry into the shade,
and the titular hero's character never develops
much independent interest. The wealth of
minor characters, of whom the country folk
are specially good, and the episodical nature
of the school-scenes, the German scenes, and
the gipsy-adventures, also tend to divert the
reader's attention, not from the father's superb
faith in his own genius and the contagion of
his personality, but from the character of the
son, who becomes little more than a pawn
upon the chess-board.

The following is an outline of the pawn's
movements.

Harry Richmond, in his childhood, resembled "a kind of shuttle-cock flying between
two battledores." He had the worst possible
training for a child, an existence divided
between two parties in his family. This unsat-

isfactory state of matters came about as follows.
His father, a music-master, had eloped with
one of the two daughters of Squire Beltham of
Riversley in Hampshire. The marriage proved
unfortunate.   The lady's fortune was squan-
dered, and she was driven crazy before her
death.   Harry, the only child of the marriage,
was taken to Riversley, where his grandfather
and aunt brought him up, for four years.

Roy Richmond, however, had plans for his
little son. Richmond was the son of an actress,
Anastasia Dewsbury, but he firmly believed
that his father had been one of the Royal Family, and he therefore determined to claim royal
honours for his son. He called himself Augustus Fitzgeorge Frederick William Richmond
Guelph Roy.   Meredith portrays him as an
unselfish, chivalrous, and warm-hearted man,
with irresistible powers of fascination, who
deceives even himself.   He is voluble and vol-
atile, half a charlatan, incorrigibly dramatic,*

* He tells how he used to stand, as a boy, beside his nurse-washer-
woman's tub, "blowing bubbles and listening to her prophecies of my
fortune for hours " (ch. xxxix).   This is one of the significant little touches
which Meredith loves to put in, casually.   Another is to be found in the
44th chapter of "The Egoist," where Lady Isabel recalls how Willoughby,
as a child, one day mounted a chair and told the family, "I am the sun of
the house."

George Meredith

a spendthrift of the first water, and an impostor on the grand scale. Roy's egotism is of a glorified character. There is a plausible, radiant gaiety about him which overpowers even his son's judgment till nearly the end of the tale, and which prevails with not a few women of his acquaintance. Goethe once wrote:

Vom Vater hab' ich die Statur,
Des Lebens ernstes Führen.

Whatever steady control of life belonged to Harry Richmond, he did not inherit it from his flamboyant sire.

The novel opens with a scene in which Roy carries off Harry from Riversley. The boy is five years old, and, after a short time in London, he is sent finally to school. Meantime Roy is off abroad, after financial troubles in London. Harry runs away from school, but is rescued from some gipsies by his aunt, and taken home to Riversley, where he is educated on the tacit understanding that he is heir to the estate, if he breaks with his father. Telemachus, however, yearns for Ulysses. From a stray hint Harry infers that his father is in London, and, in company with Temple,

The Adventures of Harry Richmond

a school-friend, he decamps for the metropolis. In a fog and a crowd, the pair are kidnapped by a philanthropic sea-captain, who fancies they have fallen into bad company and thinks a voyage will bring them to their senses. On board the "Priscilla,"* in spite of their protestations, they are carried to Germany, where they manage to make their way to a small German court. Here Roy is found, match-making on Harry's behalf, whom he represents not only as "the grandson and heir of one of the richest commoners in England" but, in addition, as possessed of royal blood, and therefore a suitable match for princess Ottilia, a little, sensible fairy of twelve or thirteen.

Father and son then return to England *vià* Paris, "the central hotel on the high-road of civilization." The squire welcomes Harry back to Riversley, while Roy's career in London again lands him in prison for debt. After being released, by the aid of Harry, the incorrigible spendthrift displays himself at

---

* The one touch of unreality in these clever chapters (xii—xiii) is the statement that two small schoolboys could recollect enough Cicero and Seneca to refute their captor's theological arguments.

George Meredith

Bath,* where a Welsh heiress falls in love with him. This escapade, from which he emerges scatheless, opens Harry's eyes to his father's scheming character, but the lad's love and pride are unaffected; in fact, the very contempt of the squire for Roy accentuates the son's obstinate determination to side with his erratic sire. On his twenty-first birthday, Harry inherits his grandmother's fortune and is promised by the squire estates and money to the value of £20,000 a year on the day when he marries Miss Jane Ilchester, the squire's protégée. In fulfilment of an old promise, however, he rejoins his father, who carries him off to Ostend, where the princess is recruiting after an illness. Harry's love for Ottilia and his affection for his father induce him to furnish the latter with funds to take the princess for a cruise in a yacht, which ends in a visit to Sarkfeld. Here the love-affair between Ottilia and Harry is wrecked, not only by her relatives' interference, but by Roy's attempt to en-

* It is in one of these chapters, the twenty-second, that the famous "leg" is brought forward, which afterwards was used with such serio-comic effect in "The Egoist."

The Adventures of Harry Richmond

trap* the former into a formal engagement ;
the girl's self-respect is wounded, and Harry
returns sadly to England with his father, and
to Riversley without him. Ere long the
story of the German affair leaks out, for
Richmond is in the field again, vaunting the
alliance between his son and Ottilia. The
squire discovers, to his disgust, that Harry's
money has been at the disposal of Roy. All
remonstrances with the latter fail. He is
infatuated by the opportunity of gaining
money to push his claim to royal birth on
behalf of Harry, and thus to forward his
interests at Sarkfeld. The invincible *bonhomie*
of the man leads him to venture on another
social flight in London, where his ambitious
follies drive the squire to exasperation and
even alarm Harry. Roy gets the latter elected
M.P. for Chippenden, and receives a
mysterious gift of £25,000, which relieves him
from serious embarrassment. This money is
really paid by the self-sacrificing, devoted
Dorothy Beltham, who has supplied him
secretly with funds all along, but Roy, in his

* The device of a love-scene overheard had been already used in
"Sandra Belloni" (ch. xxxvi),

George Meredith

infatuation, takes the gift as a tacit attempt
on the part of Royalty to hush up his claim.
His manœuvres therefore become more pronounced than ever. He inveigles Princess
Ottilia over to the Isle of Wight, by sending
an exaggerated report of Harry's health, and
apparently has the threads of the plot in his
own hands. But the entanglement fails.
The meshes of the net break. Harry realises *
that Ottilia cannot be won in this underhand
fashion, or indeed at all; she herself is too
high-minded to let Roy, " the hopping, skip-
ping social meteor, weaver of webs," manage
her destiny; her relatives interfere in time to
safeguard the honour of her name, which
Roy imagined could only be saved by her
marriage to his son; the Squire and Janet
appear on the scene, and side with the
princess; finally, in a tremendous interview,
Roy is denounced and exposed by the indignant squire as an impostor, a blackguard, and
a swindler.

The squire only lives for eight months after

* " This looking at the roots of yourself, if you are possessed of a nobler
half that will do it, is a sound corrective of an excessive ambition. Unfortunately it would seem that young men can do it only in sickness "
(ch. xlvii).

this. Janet inherits all his property, while £3,000 a year is Harry's comparatively slender portion. The latter devotes himself to his father, whose spirits are shattered, though he never whines over the collapse of his ambitions. Ottilia marries a German prince, and Harry, still sore at what he is conceited enough to consider Janet's hard treatment of himself, goes off to travel on the Continent,* returning to find Janet engaged to the Marquis of Edbury, a vicious young aristocrat. He then realises the sterling worth of this adorable English girl and the depth of his real feeling for her. But it is too late. On the eve of the marriage, however, the Marquis is killed, and Harry eventually wins Janet under Ottilia's roof. They go back to England, only to find Riversley on fire, and Roy burned to death.

This novel is one of the easiest to read in all the series of the Meredith-romances. It is a study in one form of social ambition, but in a sense there is more adventure in it than in

* " Carry your fever to the Alps, you of minds diseased." The passage at the close of ch. liii, beginning with these words, is paralleled by the Alpine scenes in " Diana of the Crossways " (ch. xv—xvi) and partially in " Beauchamp's Career " (ch. xlvi, at the beginning).

George Meredith

most of the others, and considerably less intrusion of philosophic comment. Now and again the author pulls himself up with the reflection: "My English tongue admonishes me that I have fallen upon a tone resembling one who uplifts the finger of piety in a salon of conversation." *But as a rule incident and action abound; in fact, as has been already hinted, they abound to the detriment of the story's construction.

Among the interspersed comments, particularly in the German scenes, Meredith has put some of his keenest work into Dr. Julius von Karsteg's incisive criticism of the English character (ch. xxix)† and Prince Hermann's estimate of the English in India (ch. xxxiv: "The masses in India are in character elephant all over, tail to proboscis! servile till they trample you, and not so stupid as they look. But you've done wonders in

---

* This semi-serious apology, in ch. xxxii, follows a profound passage upon the influence of the past. "We are sons of yesterday, not of the morning. The past is our mortal mother, no dead thing."

† With the description of plutocrats as "huge human pumpkins, who cover your country and drain its blood and intellect," compare the use of the gourd in "Beauchamp's Career" (ch. xxv). The swollen, ungainly pumpkin is a favourite Meredithian symbol for rich vapidity and selfishness.

The Adventures of Harry Richmond

in India, and we can't forget it. Your administration of justice is worth all your battles there"), the latter recurring in "Lord Ormont and his Aminta" more than once. The great descriptive passages are in chapters ii and iii, where Harry's boyhood is delineated, in ch. xi (the fog in London), in ch. xv (the meeting with Ottilia in the forest), in ch. xxx (the love-scene beside the lake), and in ch. xlvi (Harry's convalescence among the gipsies). In the last-named chapter, Meredith contrasts Kiomi* with some other members of her sex. "Chastity of nature, intense personal pride, were as proper to her as the free winds are to the heaths: they were as visible to dull divination as the milky blue about the iris of her eyeballs. She had actually no animal vileness, animal though she might be termed, and would have appeared if compared with Heriot's admirable Cissies and Gwennies, and other ladies of the Graces that run to fall, and spend their pains more in kindling the scent of the huntsman than in effectively flying." The said

* She belongs to the line which runs from the "Gitanilla" of Cervantes to Hugo's "Esmeralda" and Borrow's "Isopel Berners."

George Meredith

Heriot and the Marquis of Edbury divide the rôle of Steerforth, and it takes both Heriot and Temple to do for Harry what Ripton does for Richard Feverel, or even little Collett for Matthew Weyburn. The gipsy girl, Kiomi, and the beautiful, vivacious Julia Rippenger* are more living than Mabel Sweetwinter, the Em'ly of the story, but Martha Thresher and Mrs. Waddy are moulded out of the same brown wholesome clay as Mrs. Boulby and Mrs. Sumfit in " Rhoda Fleming." Mrs. Waddy's subservience to Roy, in fact, is the glorification of Mrs. Todger's reverential attitude to Mr. Pecksniff.† As for the squire, Meredith has sketched in him "the Tory mind, in its attachment to solidity, fixity, certainty, its unmatched generosity within a limit, its devotion to the family, and its family eye for the country," but in his next novel he was to draw another type of this sturdy, loyal character, upon more heroic lines, in the

* The love-passages between her and Heriot at school are echoed in the opening scenes of " Lord Ormont and his Aminta."

† "Give me leave to tell you it requires a most penetrating eye to discern a fool through the disguises of gaiety and good breeding." Fielding gives this saying to a woman ("Tom Jones," book xi, ch. 5).

The Adventures of Harry Richmond

Earl of Romfrey. It is one proof of the writer's skill that, while we sympathise with the squire in his contempt and anger, the exposure of Roy leaves us with a certain pity for the poor wretch. Mr. Peterborough, the clerical tutor, is treated with the same deadly sarcasm as his fellow clergymen in the rest of the novels; he is a pompous and amorous lay-figure. The Bulsted brothers are a refined, upper-class type of the farcical pair in "Evan Harrington."

Pride and sentimentalism, as usual, are among the dominant motives of the tale. Harry has a pride of his own, in his fancied sense of mastery over the squire and of penetration into Janet's real character, as well as in the craving for "the vain glitter of hereditary distinction" (ch. xxxiii), which he caught from Roy, but the sentimentalism of his nonsensical airs is equally marked. He allows his dreams of his father and his romantic attachment to Ottilia to interfere with his better judgment, till they blind him to the real facts of the case. As he confesses, he was an egotist. His self-love was his worst enemy. "I remember walking at my swiftest pace, blaming everybody I knew for insufficiency, for want of subordination to my interests, for poverty of nature, grossness, blindness to the fine lights shining in me ; I blamed the Fates for harassing me, circumstances for not surrounding me with friends worthy of me. The central *I* resembled the sun of this universe, with the difference that it shrieked for nourishment, instead of dispensing it. My monstrous conceit of elevation will not suffer condensation into sentences." It is the carnival of egotism which occurs in the love-season of youth.

Like Evan Harrington, Harry is brought to his senses by the influence of good and true women. Janet Ilchester read him more truly than Princess Ottilia,* and while the character of the latter is drawn in exquisite half-lines, it is the English girl who develops better. Meredith makes her a woman of courage and sense. From "a bold, plump girl, fond of male society," she grows into a splendid Englishwoman, self-reliant and shrewd, "as

* As later in "The Egoist," so here, Meredith shows how two women, interested in the same man, are able to avoid suspicion of one another, if they are large-hearted enough. The relations between Lady Charlotte and Emilia, in "Sandra Belloni," are similar but inferior.

firm as a rock and as sweet as a flower on it."
Ottilia is more elusive. She is apparently in
love with Harry, but courage is required to
bring their love to a point, and her traditions
and training handicap her. She has not even
the help of finding courage in Harry, who
misses her as Beauchamp missed Renée.
"She was a woman who could only love
intelligently—love, that is, in the sense of
giving herself. She had the power of passion,
and it could be stirred ; but he who kindled it
wrecked his chance if he could not stand clear
in her intellect's unsparing gaze." Ottilia,
especially after her illness, let her romantic
imagination dwell on Harry ; but her native
sense soon controlled the generous sentiment
of her heart, and she was saved from what
would have been a mésalliance by her perception of Roy's scheming * and of Harry's
weaknesses. At the same time, her marriage
to the German prince is left unexplained,

---

* One of Roy's ejaculations recalls a sentence in "The Ordeal of Richard
Feverel." When he is baffled by the straightforwardness of Lieschen, a
German maid, he apostrophises the untameable things of life as "Idiots,
insects, women, and the salt sea ocean !" Meredith had already remarked
that "argument with Mrs. Doria was like firing paper-pellets against a
stone-wall."

George Meredith

as is Janet's engagement to the Marquis Edbury. The episode of the election (in ch. xliii) is equally loose ; but in his next novel Meredith was to lift English politics into a really central place, just as he was to draw at full length in Cecilia Halkett the figure which he had merely outlined in Clara Goodwin.

BEAUCHAMP'S CAREER

Beauchamp's Career

IN 1868 Meredith assisted his friend, Captain Frederick Maxse, R.N., who was standing as Radical candidate for Southampton after a brilliant phase of service in the Crimea. "Beauchamp's Career," first published in book-form in 1876, was an outcome of this electioneering experience. Captain (afterwards Admiral) Maxse was one of the author's closest friends; "Modern Love" had been dedicated to him in 1862; and it was this personal friendship which lent such glow to the delineation of Nevil Beauchamp's character and also helped to make the novel one of the richest in the Meredith-series. The author frankly confesses it is a political novel, but the reader need not be afraid. This is neither a viewy nor a dull book; it is political in the sense that all questions of social reform and imperial policy are viewed through the vivid, engaging

George Meredith

temperament of a personality.* The book has no plot. Nevil Beauchamp's career seems to be opening just when he is drowned. But the episodes of the sailor - politician's life can be arranged so as to throw light upon his development, more easily than in the case of "Vittoria," which is equally plotless.

The outline of events is as follows.

Nevil Beauchamp is an orphan; his father, a colonel in the British army, had married the eldest sister of the Hon. Everard Romfrey, of Steynham in Sussex, a sturdy aristocrat. Nevil had become a midshipman, and when the story opens his chivalrous temper is excited on behalf of his country, which is threatened by a French invasion.† He also fights a young cousin, Cecil Baskelett, for casting reflections upon the name of Mrs.

---

* "I give you the position of the country . . . The youth I introduce to you will rarely let us escape from it; for the reason that he was born with so extreme and passionate a love for his country, that he thought all things else of mean importance in comparison."

† The prose version of the panic in 1853 will be found in Morley's "Life of Cobden" (ch. xxiii). The third and fourth chapters of the novel should be read along with the twenty-fourth chapter of the same biography.

Beauchamp's Career

Rosamund Culling,* the widow of an English officer, who keeps house for his uncle, and who has a warm, maternal love for the boy. When the Crimean war breaks out, he agrees with Bright and the Manchester school—to his uncle's disgust. But, when ordered to the Dardanelles, he behaves pluckily. A French friend, Captain Roland de Croisnel, takes him to Venice, to recover from a wound, and there he falls madly in love with his friend's sister, a lovely girl of seventeen. Roland owes his life to Nevil, and the girl's gratitude presently ripens, under the subtle charm of the place and of Beauchamp's personality, into a warmer feeling. Renée, however, has been already promised by her father to a middle-aged French count, who appears upon the scene. She refuses,† after

---

* One of Richardson's lady-correspondents pled with him to make a widow the heroine of a story. "I wish to see an exemplary widow drop from your pen." Rosamund Culling is Meredith's nearest approach to this, for Lady Blandish and Lady Grace Halley are secondary figures; Mrs. Chump is out of the question, and the rest are either not exemplary or unimportant. He never challenged the laurels won by Thackeray in "Esmond."

† Lack of courage at Venice, as afterwards at Tourdestelle, prevents her from breaking through conventionalities; but Meredith also mentions the sense of duty to her family. He was in love with this Frenchwoman among his heroines, and the reader is almost inclined to share his feelings towards her.

George Meredith

a passionate love-scene with Nevil (in the
glorious chapters viii and ix), to obey the
instincts of her heart and marry the English
officer. Nevil's appeals by letter to his uncle
only provoke the latter's amusement, and,
instead of returning to settle in England, he
goes off cruising in the Mediterranean on a
war-ship, and serves with distinction on the
African coast. He is made commander.
When he does return to England, it is to
stand as Radical candidate for Bevisham,
under the ægis of a Dr. Shrapnel, aged
eighty-six, who is a single-minded Radical
agitator against game-laws, land-laws, creeds,
and marriage-laws.

Everard Romfrey, annoyed at this breach in
the family traditions of Toryism, puts up Cecil
Baskelett, now an idle, mischievous army
officer, as the rival candidate. At the height
of the canvass, an enigmatic message from
Renée summons Beauchamp to Tourdestelle,
her country-seat in France, where she had
boasted to a young admirer about her English
friend's chivalry, and had staked her glove that
he would respond to her summons within a
specified term of hours. As a storm had delayed

214

him beyond his time, the glove is forfeited, but Beauchamp recovers it, outwits his French rival, and returns to England, leaving Renée as he had found her, a neglected, unhappy wife. Her whim costs Nevil his election. The repeated rumours of an intrigue with a Frenchwoman ruin his chances, and he is at the bottom of the poll. He also endangers his chances in another direction. Miss Cecilia Halkett, the daughter of an English colonel, an heiress, a yachtswoman, and a beauty, finds it harder than ever to champion her friend Beauchamp against the persistent gossip of the county, while the glamour of Renée prevents him from doing justice to the splendid qualities of the English girl's character.* Mrs. Culling does her best to open his eyes to his opportunity. His uncle favours the match, and even Renée writes, advising him to marry. He does make a move towards Cecilia. But matters are suddenly twisted by an unscrupulous action† on the

---

* A more creditable scruple also swayed him; he was at this time in need of money (see ch. xxxix).

† Done under the influence of liquor; but it was bad wine, Meredith explains!

part of Captain Baskelett, who misrepresents Dr. Shrapnel to Everard Romfrey as having reflected on Mrs. Culling's character. Romfrey's anger leads him to horsewhip the doctor,* for which Nevil insists that he must apologise. Romfrey, however, appeals to Mrs. Culling for proof that Shrapnel had previously insulted her, when she went to remonstrate with him for entangling Nevil. She has not courage to confess that her personal dislike for Shrapnel had led her to exaggerate the doctor's language into an untruth, giving Romfrey a wrong impression of him. Her weakness has the effect of confirming Romfrey in his refusal to apologise, and of embittering Nevil against his uncle and herself. "You set fire to the train," the indignant youth tells her. "You hated the old man, and you taught Mr. Romfrey to think you had been insulted. I see it all. Now you must have the courage to tell him of your error." His very courtship of Cecilia

---

* He does not describe the horsewhipping, any more than Wilfrid's castigation of Mr. Pericles in "Sandra Belloni"; even the account in "One of Our Conquerors" (ch. xxxvii) is bare and allusive. Similarly with the duels throughout the novels: Meredith often discusses them, but he never describes them, although they are sometimes vital to his plot.

Beauchamp's Career

is subordinated to the desire of exacting an apology from Everard.

The unexpected succession of the latter to the title of Lord Avonley only whets Beauchamp's zeal, until his uncle is stung into losing his temper and retorting with a demand that Beauchamp shall apologise to Mrs. Culling; when the youth refuses, he is ordered to leave the family house in London which he had been allowed to tenant. Suddenly Renée appears in London, flying in desperation from her husband to throw herself on Nevil's protection. But, like Clotilde in "The Tragic Comedians," she is taken aback. She finds that her lover wishes prudently to safeguard her position, before taking any rash step, instead of impetuously carrying her off.* He telegraphs for Mrs. Culling to chaperon her, and her family are summoned, like Princess Ottilia's in "The Adventures of Harry Richmond," to safeguard her reputation.

---

* Besides, Shrapnel's ethical teaching upon the danger of passion interfering with duty had borne fruit. "He could not possibly talk to her, who had cast the die, of his later notions of morality and the world's dues, fees, and claims on us." "A man standing against the world in a good cause, with a runaway wife on his hands, carries a burden, however precious it be to him." But he cannot admit this scruple to the runaway herself!

George Meredith

Renée, half against her will, is again saved from herself by Beauchamp. Before the French party leave, Lord Avonley at last manages to persuade Mrs. Culling to marry him, while Cecilia, at the fresh evidence of what seems to be Beauchamp's persistent infatuation for Renée, feels it unmaidenly to let her heart go out to him any longer. She and her father start for Italy ; on her return she agrees to marry a Mr. Blackburn Tuckham, who has been persistently wooing her. She has no sooner done so than Beauchamp arrives to propose to her on his own account. After a last interview they part, she bitterly reproaching herself for having ever doubted him, he stunned by the loss of a woman whom he had only learned to appreciate rightly when it was too late.

Meantime Lady Avonley, who is expecting her first child,* is broken-hearted at Nevil's loss of Cecilia, and blames herself bitterly for her cowardice in having failed to give her husband a true account of Shrapnel's conduct

---

* This is the third instance of Meredith's insight into the effects produced by maternity upon a woman's character. He had touched the same string in describing Lucy Feverel and Vittoria Ammiani, and he was to do so again, with even greater power, in Carinthia Fleetwood.

Beauchamp's Career

towards herself. She sets herself to persuade the Earl to make an apology. The news of Nevil's illness swells her eagerness; she plans to apologise herself; and eventually her husband, in order to pacify her, bends his pride and apologises handsomely to Dr. Shrapnel.

This is the emotional climax of the story. The last two chapters huddle up the closing events of the career of Beauchamp. On recovering from his illness he marries Jenny Denham, the doctor's ward, who has been his nurse. The marriage is one of gratitude, rather than of love, but the pair are happy together during their brief married life. It is brief, for, a year later, Beauchamp is drowned in the Otley, when rescuing a little boy.

The gratuitous tragedy of Beauchamp's death lies open to the same shafts of criticism as fell upon the conclusion of "The Ordeal of Richard Feverel." But it is thankless to dwell on any such flaws of construction when the novel offers a wealth of pregnant insight and romance which is unrivalled in the entire series of the Meredithian stories. It is not a one-figure book, by any means, but the hero's

George Meredith

character * is the outstanding feature of its
pages. Beauchamp is a young naval officer
of the best type, full of spirit, keen on his
profession, chivalrous,† and tenacious of his
purpose. What deflects him, like Alvan, is
the disturbing element of passion. In his
romantic adoration of Renée Meredith marks
the danger of passion being stirred too early,
when the nature is apt to be swayed beyond
the control of reason. Eve came too soon
upon the scene. Beauchamp's love is no
mere susceptibility to the charms of women.
He remains loyal to Renée. But while his
nature is not inflammable, it is described as
thrown out of its proper balance and harmony
by the entrance of this love-passion for the
French girl. Strongly as Meredith empha-
sises the truth that a capacity for being stirred
and moved by passion forms an element of all
growth, he is thoroughly alive to the risk of
it breaking loose from the sovereign brain.
One of the most unfortunate results of this

* He begins on the good foundation of hero-worship, not only for men
of action but for men of ideas like Carlyle. This saves him from being
conceited and priggish, even in his youthful propaganda against the Toryism of his relations.

† He inherited this from his father (see ch. xxvi).

Beauchamp's Career

aberration, in the case of Beauchamp, is the injustice which he does to himself and to Cecilia Halkett.* She is wasted upon Mr. Blackburn Tuckham, a dogmatic, exuberant Tory with "a round head, square flat forehead, and ruddy face; he stood as if his feet claimed the earth under them for his own." The comic spirit revels in this type of Englishman. Every touch tells. "On the question of politics, 'I venture to state,' he remarked in anything but the tone of a venture, 'that no educated man of ordinary sense who has visited our colonies will come back a Liberal.' As for a man of sense and education being a Radical, he scouted the notion with a pooh sufficient to awaken a vessel in the doldrums." Mr. Tuckham still walks on the grain-giving earth, though the Cecilia Halketts of real life are more likely to throw themselves away on detestable, plausible army captains like

---

* She had all the makings of a true mate for Beauchamp. In ch. xxxiv, after describing her fresh, graceful beauty, Meredith gives her this keen saying: "Intellectual differences do not cause wounds, except when very unintellectual sentiments are behind'them :—my conceit, your impatience." Impatience was Beauchamp's defect. Cecilia's was not conceit, whatever it may have been; feminine prejudice in her, as in Mrs. Culling, is responsible for mistakes of judgment, but Meredith draws her quick-witted, warm, high-spirited, and noble character in colours which leave her only second to Diana among the Englishwomen of the novels.

221

Cecil Baskelett than on dry politicians. Tuckham, however, was a gentleman ; and he had more ideas than Mr. Caddis or than Sir Twickenham Pryme, who bored the Misses Pole with his mangold-wurzel and statistics. Meredith drew him partly from his old and valued friend, Sir William Hardman, editor of the " Morning Post."

The second weakness in the youth's character was the intolerance produced by the domination of a single idea.* Meredith shows (especially in ch. xxxviii) how he got irritated by opposition, and irritated instead of conciliating others, the reason being that he had "given up his brains for a lodging to a single idea. It is at once a devouring dragon and an intractable steam force. Inspired of solitude and gigantic size it claims divine origin." In Nevil's case, it prevented him from doing justice to his opponents, and it led him to consider Cecilia less as a woman than as a splendid prize to be cut out by means of Radical argument from under the guns of the

---

* This *motif* recurs in " One of Our Conquerors," but it is also noted in "The Amazing Marriage" (see Carinthia's confession to Rebecca Wythan in ch. xxx).

Tory fort. Cecilia evidently shared Lady Mary Montagu's opinion that politics and controversy were as unbecoming to the sex as the dress of a prizefighter. She wanted love not logic.*

The real strength of Beauchamp lay in (*a*) his fine public spirit. "He questioned his justification, and yours, for gratifying tastes in an ill-regulated world of wrong-doing, suffering, sin, and bounties unrighteously dispensed —not sufficiently dispersed." A true aristocracy, he held, should lead the people, instead of lolling in luxury. (*b*) He had also brains, and used them. (*c*) He was not a sentimentalist, though he was an idealist. "Beauchampism may be said to stand for nearly everything which is the obverse of Byronism, and shuns the statuesque pathetic, or any kind of posturing." Meredith is much fairer to Byron than, e.g., Peacock ever could bring himself to be, but Byronism he derided on all occasions, and Beauchamp serves as its natural foil.

* When she defended, for argument's sake partly, her inherited Toryism, he felt she was "not yet so thoroughly mastered as to grant her husband his just prevalence with her"!

George Meredith

Ten years earlier, George Eliot had published her political novel, but, while "Felix
Holt" and "Beauchamp's Career" both turn
upon the same problem, viz., the love-inter-
ests of a young man as these are affected by
pre-occupation in political and social reforms,
the heroes differ widely. Felix Holt is a
Radical of the 1832 period, Beauchamp belongs
to an age twenty years later. The one is a
fiery Glasgow student, the other a naval
officer; the one is lacking in masculine fibre,
whereas Beauchamp is never mawkish;
Beauchamp, too, is the chivalrous gentleman
throughout, even when he bores Cecilia and
remonstrates with Mrs. Culling hotly, while
Felix Holt plies Esther with rude taunts upon
her pretensions to be a fine lady.

Meredith's sympathies are obvious here, as
in "Vittoria," but in both novels he writes
with impartial justice. The Liberal spouter,
Timothy Turbot, and the incorruptible (!)
Radical, Tomkins, are painted as faithfully as
the brainless Tory aristocrats; the political
analysis wrings the withers of Liberal, Tory,
and Radical alike. The election is described
with more lavish detail than in "The Adven-

tures of Harry Richmond," and the description contains far more than humorous incidents or the stock-in-trade of the subject. Dr. Shrapnel's letter, and indeed his conversation throughout the novel, simply epitomise the characteristic opinions which Meredith voices in "The Empty Purse," "Foresight and Patience," "The Old Chartist," "Aneurin's Harp," "To Colonel Charles," "England Before the Storm," "A Faith on Trial," "Hard Weather," and "The Test of Manhood." One of the fairest criticisms of Shrapnel is put into the mouth of Seymour Austin, who thus defines the politics of impatience. "He perceives a bad adjustment of things; which is correct. He is honest, and takes his honesty for a virtue: and that entitles him to believe in himself: and that belief causes him to see in all opposition to him the wrong he has perceived in existing circumstances: and so in a dream of power he invokes the people: and as they do not stir, he takes to prophecy."

The wonderful love-scenes on the Adriatic and at Venice are an expansion of the hints in Vittoria (ch. xxx), where " Ammiani

o 225

George Meredith

remembered his having stood once on the Lido of Venice, and eyed the dawn across the Adriatic, and dreamed that Violetta was born of the loveliness and held in her bosom the hopes of morning," and also in "The Ordeal of Richard Feverel" where Richard dreamed of floating with Bella in a gondola "past grand old towers, colossal squares, gleaming quays, and out and on with her, on into the silver infinity shaking over seas." Incidentally, Meredith throws in a number of edged aphorisms (e.g. "Shrugging and sneering is about as honourable as blazing fireworks over your own defeat," and "most of our spiritual guides neglect the root to trim the flower"), states his views on journalism * (ch. xliv), on the English church (chs. xvii and xxix) and the clergy in general (ch. lvi), on luxury and wealth, and on the army and navy. The various descriptions of the women's beauty (e.g. "Cecilia was a more beautiful woman than Renée : but on which does the eye linger longest—which draws the heart? a radiant landscape, where the tall ripe wheat flashes

---

* Compare Lytton's treatment of Mr. Jack Tibbets in "The Caxtons."

between shadow and shine in the stately march of Summer, or the peep into dewy woodland on to dark water?"), the account of Carlyle's style (ch. ii) * and of John Bright (ch. iv), the subtle analysis of chapters xl—xlii, and the yachting-scenes † (especially that in ch. xv), are all examples of the author's versatility and rare powers of imagination. The allusion to women ("who dare not be spontaneous. This is their fate, only in degree less inhuman than that of Hellenic and Trojan princesses offered up to the Gods") in ch. xxxii, by the way, is repeated in the next novel (see the end of ch. xliii of "The Egoist"). Seymour Austin (see the character-isation in ch. xxxix) is modelled on the lines of Merthyr Powys, but unfortunately we get too little of him and his conversation. Stukely Culbrett, again, is kept within limits more successfully than his more acid fellow-satirist, Colney Durance, in "One of Our Conquerors."

In the original version of ch. liv, Jenny

* There is a fine tribute to Carlyle's humour in "The Essay on Comedy."

† Nevil is a more expert yachtsman than Richard Feverel or Redworth, naturally.

George Meredith

Denham, who is one of the first-rate musical amateurs in Meredith, plays the ninth symphony of Beethoven on the piano. This would be strong meat even for a musical enthusiast in good health, and Beauchamp was neither the one (see ch. xxxii) nor the other. But it would require a full orchestra and chorus. Besides, it would take up a whole evening. In response to friendly remonstrances, the author has restricted Jenny in the later editions to selections from the aforesaid symphony.

Meredith makes Jenny Denham walk "like a yacht before the wind." He is fond of comparing ships and girls, and there is more about the sea in this story than in any of its predecessors. Cecilia "loved the sea, and the stinging salt spray, and circling gull and plunging gurnet, the sun on the waves and the torn cloud." To love Beauchamp, as she did, was like being at sea in a storm. The sea is more than an apt background for several of the episodes, however. It symbolises the vitality and freshness and pulse of the ideas which surge through the novel. "Beauchamp's Career" is a clever book, but

228

cleverness is the last thing we think about as
we read its pages. It is an ennobling and
inspiriting book, and a large part of its
attractiveness lies in the delineation of human
nature in contact with the surge and spray of
deep elemental forces in the modern world.
In his next great novel Meredith was to bend,
with keen eyes, over an inland pool.

THE HOUSE ON THE BEACH

The House on the Beach

THIS "realistic tale," published in "The New Quarterly Magazine" for January, 1877, is a study in the social ambitions of a tradesman. The hero, a fussy, local magistrate, recalls the type satirised by Dickens in Mr. Nupkins of "The Pickwick Papers," but he is used by Meredith to illustrate the absurdity and mischief of social aspirations. The desire to mount in the scale of society leads to affectation, unreality, unhappiness, and the breaking of old, true ties: such is the burden of this story, as of "Rhoda Fleming" and "Sandra Belloni" especially. "The land is in a state of fermentation to mount." Meredith, like Thackeray before him, satirises in particular the effort to throw off the name of tradesman as he had already done at greater length in "Evan Harrington," although "satirises" is hardly the right word to use in this connexion, for in Herbert Fellingham Meredith shows

233

once more the futility of mere satire as a corrective power in human life, just as in Mrs. Crickledon, the joiner's wife, he draws a picture of the sensible, common woman, which recalls the more important sketch of Mrs. Berry.

Mr. Mart Tinman is a retired tradesman who has become bailiff of Crikswich, one of the Cinque Ports. He resides with his widowed sister in a house on the beach "posted where it stood, one supposes, for the sake of the sea-view, from which it turned right about to face the town across a patch of grass and salt scurf, looking like a square and scornful corporal engaged in the perpetual review of an awkward squad of recruits." Tinman has strong social ambitions. He has retired from business at the age of 40, in the hope of marrying "a born lady," but his matrimonial aims have failed ; Tinman is handicapped fatally by his low birth, an uncertainty about his h's, and his bad wine. When the story opens, he is trying another tack. He is anxious to present an address to the Queen, congratulating her in the name of the Port on the betrothal of one of the

The House on the Beach

princesses, and, in order to practise his gestures, hires a cheval-glass before which to pose in court-dress. This occupation leaves him too busy and too proud to welcome his rich old friend, Van Diemen Smith, who has returned from Australia with his daughter Annette, in order to settle in the old country. Van Diemen Smith is an *alias* for Philip Ribstone, who had deserted from the army years before in order to protect his wife's honour; but this secret is known only to Tinman, for whom the Australian has a sentimental and loyal affection. His chivalrous good-nature is wounded by Tinman's cool reception, but, after some squabbling, he settles down in the neighbourhood.

Meantime Annette is courted by a young journalist, Herbert Fellingham, whose satirical spirit is resented by the others. He makes merciless fun of Tinman's address, and thereby ruins his chances of winning Annette, for Smith's simple, good-nature is offended by the caricaturing of his friend. The differences between the two men, however, grow more pronounced. Smith outbids Tinman at sales, thwarts his public policy, and ventures even to praise Australia at the expense of England. The bailiff's narrow, envious nature resents this implicit depreciation of himself. "His main grievance against Van Diemen was the non-recognition of his importance by that uncultured Australian, who did not seem to be conscious of the dignities and distinctions we come to in our country." In order to gratify his wounded pride, he threatens to expose Smith to the War Office as a deserter. He thus has the Australian in his power, and, eager to secure a hold upon his ducats and his daughter, he meanly employs this lever to further his suit to Annette, who feels herself obliged to favour Tinman's wooing, in order to safeguard her father's interests. Fellingham begins to suspect the truth, from certain hints dropped in conversation, but no outsider's aid is needed ; Tinman precipitates the issue by his own spiteful temper. Irritated at the delay and obstinacy of Smith in the matter of the marriage, he writes a letter to the Horse Guards, giving information about Smith's past. But the house is destroyed that night by a storm and a high tide, and the

The House on the Beach

letter, rescued by the maid-servant, is opened by Smith, who thus discovers his friend's treachery. Fellingham had already told him that the threat was not nearly so serious as he feared, and the revelation merely proved to him the meanness and petty nature of his quondam comrade. Thus the house on the beach collapses, and with it the vulgar and pretentious authority claimed by Tinman over Crikswich and his friend. The end of the story is rather huddled up—a not uncommon fault in Meredith—but in the last paragraph he finds room to mention one of his leading ideas, viz., the wholesome effect of laughter.*

* Compare, *e.g.*, the "Ode to the Comic Spirit," and "The Appeasement of Demeter."

GENERAL OPLE
AND LADY CAMPER

The Case of General Ople
and Lady Camper

THE scene of this delicious little story,
which appeared in "The New Quarterly Magazine" for July, 1877, is laid on
the banks of the Thames, where General
Wilson Ople, a retired officer, aged fifty-
five, has taken a small villa for himself and
his young daughter Elizabeth. Next to this
"gentlemanly residence," as the General loved
to call it, stands Douro Lodge, which is subsequently rented by an eccentric, aristocratic
widow, aged forty-one. Lady Camper is of
Welsh blood, and, like Lady Eglett in "Lord
Ormont and his Aminta," she is one of those
ladies in whom Meredith delights to show
how an active brain and high spirit are com-
patible with middle age. The point of the
tale is the relationship between this clever,
keen woman and the simple soldier at her
gates. The latter cherishes deferential and
obsequious feelings towards the aristocracy.

George Meredith

He is also shy and susceptible, so far as women are concerned, and he is intensely sensitive to ridicule. "Clever women alarmed and paralysed him. Their aptness to question and require immediate sparkling answers; their demand for fresh wit, of a kind that is not furnished by publications which strike it into heads with a hammer, and supply it wholesale; their various reading; their power of ridicule too; made them awful in his contemplation." The General is becoming self-satisfied, and rather vain, however. Egoism is preventing him, for example, from realising that his daughter and Mr. Reginald Rolles, a nephew of Lady Camper, have fallen in love. Observing this, Lady Camper proceeds to take her inflammable and gallant neighbour in hand, in order to weed him of his selfishness. Presently she reduces him, by a mixture of haughtiness and friendliness, to an abject state of slavery. Her aim is to rouse him to consideration for his daughter's happiness and prospects, but the infatuated officer, hoodwinked by his egoism, interprets her remarks on marriage as advances to himself. In order to punish

him, as well as to make a fresh attempt to
stir his fatherly instincts, Lady Camper
leaves for the Continent, and the poor
General is persecuted by a series of merciless
caricatures of himself. These, drawn and
posted by his witty neighbour, drive the
sensitive man nearly distracted, but, instead
of disgusting him, they rather fascinate him.
"It was partly her whippings of him, partly
her penetration ; her ability that sat so finely
on a wealthy woman, her indifference to conventional manners, that so well beseemed a
nobly-born one, and more than all, her
correction of his little weaknesses and in-
competencies, in spite of his dislike of it, won
him." At last she returns home and ends
the General's torture by opening his eyes to
the object of her cruel treatment, namely, a
sense of his duty to the young people. By
working on his fear of ridicule, Lady Camper
explains that she has saved him from a selfish
indifference to his daughter's happiness, and
also from the smug, suburban existence of
his neighbours, from being reduced "to the
level of the people round about us here—
who are, what? Inhabitants of gentlemanly

residences, yes ! But what kind of creatures ? They have no mental standard, no moral aim, no native chivalry." The two then marry. For Lady Camper relents. She has not only secured Elizabeth's happiness but has found in the General a husband "likely ever to be a fund of amusement for her humour, good, irrepressible, and above all, very picturesque." This merry, shrewd lady is well mated, according to Meredith's philosophy of laughter, with a man who has learned to laugh at himself for his vain idea of being " one of our conquerors."

This little piece of social comedy is a skit on social ambitions, like " The House on the Beach," but while Tinman wanted to be a gentleman, General Ople was a gentleman, or at any rate had the makings of one. The other motif of the story is equally character-istic of Meredith, viz., the need for putting aside one's private ends in order to further the interests of the next generation. The General was not a tyrant ; he was fond of his daughter ; but he was inclined to subordinate her interests to his own, and to treat her prospects as secondary to her father's, so

General Ople and Lady Camper

much so that he became indifferent to her reputation and happiness. The fuller and deeper bearings of this law of unselfishness were developed later in "The Empty Purse."

Lady Camper is one of Meredith's "crucible-women." The story of her dealings with the General shows how, next to his use of money, it is a man's conduct towards women which forms the surest test of his character.

THE TALE OF CHLOE

The Tale of Chloe

THIS short, tragic story was published
in "The New Quarterly Magazine"
for July, 1879. It is described in the sub-
title as "An episode in the history of
Beau Beamish," but it really gathers round
the experience of two women in the fashionable and artificial society of 18th century
Bath—a phase of life which Meredith had
already sketched, with inimitable touches of
mock-heroic comedy, in the twenty-first and
twenty-second chapters of "The Adventures
of Harry Richmond."

Susan Bailey, a rustic beauty, had been
suddenly lifted from the dairy to ducal rank
by marrying an elderly, and infatuated,
peer. Her mania for pleasure reduces the
Duke to his wits' end, and after three years
he finds himself obliged to appeal to Beau
Beamish, the suave autocrat of the local
society, to take charge of the young flighty

Duchess during a month's gaiety which she had been promised at the Wells. The Beau undertakes the responsibility. He is sure that he can guarantee the girl-wife a taste of society without letting her be carried off her feet. He assigns her the mocking incognito of "The Duchess of Dewlap,"* and attaches to her person, as companion, Miss Catherine Martinsward (the "Chloe" of the tale), a gentle, discreet, and noble lady, uncorrupted by the society of Bath, who had spent her fortune to pay the gambling debts of an unworthy lover, the handsome and spendthrift Sir Martin Caseldy. Her love is unrequited, but she has no reproaches for him. With the loyalty of a sound, bright nature, she lives in daily expectation of seeing Caseldy at Bath, but he treacherously refuses to reward her generosity and fulfil his word, "with a blacker brand upon him every morning that he looks forth across his property, and leaves her to languish." In spite of this ill-treatment, which has now lasted for seven years, she has neither lost

* An allusion to this story occurs in the second chapter of "The Adventures of Harry Richmond."

The Tale of Chloe

faith in him nor dropped her sprightly air
and gay spirits.

Driving out with the Beau to meet the
Duchess, Chloe recognises Caseldy in the
distance playing the cavalier to the new
arrival. He has returned to Bath at last,
but to flirt with the Duchess, not to win
Chloe. The latter's suspicions are aroused,
and when Caseldy publicly appears on the
scene, his conduct is far from reassuring
her, though he lets it be understood that he
is to marry her when her month's engagement with the Duchess is over. He and
the Duchess meet secretly. Their mutual
passion grows, whilst Chloe has to look on.
At every fresh evidence of her lover's
treachery, she ties a knot in a thick silken
skein which she carries in one hand, but
without any revengeful feelings towards
either of the pair. "She treated them both
with a proud generosity surpassing gentleness.
All that there was of selfishness in her
bosom resolved to the enjoyment of her one
month of strongly willed delusion." For,
while she has her own plan for preventing
mischief and saving her friend the Duchess,

meantime, with a tragic humility, she determines to enjoy her month of nearness to Caseldy, even though she sees through the doubleness of his conduct towards herself. Caseldy hoodwinks the Beau. But Chloe is not blind to her lover's ungenerous and treacherous behaviour. At the same time she will not remonstrate with him, any more than with his infatuated companion. "Her lover," she reflects, "would not have come to her but for his pursuit of another woman."

Presently matters are brought to a head by the Duchess and Caseldy planning to elope on the following morning at three o'clock. Chloe, who sleeps in the room next to her friend, now puts her plan in execution. She hangs herself on the door of their sitting-room by the skein she had knotted, and as the Duchess slips out she encounters this tragic obstacle to her flight. The girl's shrieks raise the house and neighbourhood, and so the elopement is effectively prevented by the despairing self-sacrifice of Chloe, that "most admirable of women, whose heart," as the Beau reflects,

The Tale of Chloe

"was broken by a faithless man ere she devoted her wreck of life to arrest one weaker than herself on the descent to perdition."

The tragic note almost jars in this little story ; self-devotion seems carried to a quixotic length in Chloe's suicide. But Meredith does not allow the sombre intensity which pervades the tale to affect the impressions of Chloe's sprightly womanhood. "She became the comrade of men without forfeit of her station among sage sweet ladies, and was like a well-mannered sparkling boy, to whom his admiring seniors have given the lead in sallies, whims, and flights ; but pleasanter than a boy, the soft hues of her sex toned her frolic spirit." These elements of true womanhood, together with an entire absence of sentimentalism, make up the attractiveness of Chloe in Meredith's long gallery of women, where her position is close to that of Dahlia Fleming.

THE EGOIST

The Egoist

THIS "comedy in narrative," published in 1879, is the study of a priggish baronet who desired to run his fiancée's mind into the mould of his own and to dominate her personality, as Sir Austin Feverel wished to do with his son. But "The Egoist" has very little action in it. The period of the comedy only lasts for a few weeks, and the vital interest of its pages lies not in what happens so much as in the desperately clever analysis of the motives which set the main characters in play. "Like Shakespere," Henley wrote, "Meredith is a man of genius, who is a clever man as well; and he seems to prefer his cleverness to his genius." This preference is visible in the psychological calculus of motives which fills the latter half of "The Egoist," in the self-consciousness of the artist, and in the laboured efforts to produce certain effects; all of which tend to complicate the reader's attitude to the story. As a matter of fact, an outline of the facts underlying this novel has perforce to be meagre. Fortunately, it is less necessary than in the case of any of the other Meredith-romances.

"He, they say, who is not handsome by Twenty, strong by Thirty, wise by Forty, rich by Fifty, will never be either handsome, strong, wise, or rich." The hero of Meredith's novel improved upon Richardson's programme of the ideal life. He was rich at twenty as well as handsome, and strong before he was thirty. Whether he was ever wise, and, if so, what was the value of his wisdom, is the problem set by the novelist to his readers.

Sir Willoughby Patterne, of Patterne Hall, is a young and wealthy aristocrat, who grows up in an atmosphere of feminine adulation. He cultivates his mind in a way, however; toys with science in a laboratory, but directs "his admirable passion to excel upon sport; and so great was the passion in him that it was commonly the presence of rivals which led him to the declaration of love." This jealousy of being outdone is responsible for

The Egoist

his engagement at the age of twenty-one to Miss Constantia Durham, who "had money, and health and beauty ; three mighty qualifications for a Patterne bride."* Sir Willoughby is one of several in pursuit of her. Like Mrs. Millamant in "The Way of the World"—one of Meredith's favourite comedies—"She had the glory of the racing cutter full sail on a winning breeze," and the danger of being outsailed by a rival induces the baronet to propose to her, although his sentimental conceit causes him a pang of regret that she has not come to him "out of cloistral purity," instead of having been admired and courted by his bugbear "the World." Miss Durham discovers his stupendous egotism in time. Ten days before the marriage, she sails away with Captain Harry Oxford, and Sir Willoughby is forced to save his face by a mild, condescending courtship of Miss Lætitia Dale,† a female adorer at his gates, who is the portionless, poetic daughter of a retired and invalid Anglo-Indian surgeon. "She was

* Sir Austin Feverel's list of names of possible brides for Richard was marked "M. or Po. or Pr." (money, position, principles).

† He pretends that Constantia was his mother's choice, and that she had been madly jealous of his true love, Lætitia !

259

pretty, her eyelashes were long and dark, her eyes dark blue, and her soul was ready to shoot like a rocket out of them at a look from Willoughby." He could count upon her as a satellite, whoever failed.

The baronet then disappears on a tour round the world, "holding an English review of his Maker's grotesques." He returns after three years to look out for a more brilliant bride than the patient Lætitia. This time it is Clara, the daughter of Rev. Dr. Middleton, a stout clerical scholar, who is a *bon vivant,* like the Dr. Gaster and Dr. Portpipe of Peacock's world.* The girl is eighteen—the same age as Aminta, when Lord Ormont wooed and married her—and she also has "money and health and beauty, the triune of perfect starriness, which makes all men astronomers." Sir Willoughby woos her hotly and carries her off from the rivals who surrounded him. Clara is too inexperienced to fathom his real character. She is not so much

---

* Peacock made partial amends for these in Dr. Opimian or in Dr. Folliott, who is nearer to Dr. Middleton than the Casaubon of "Middlemarch." Dr. Middleton is at least warm-blooded. He would have agreed with Prince Seithenyn in Peacock's tale, "wine is my medicine, and my quantity is a little more."

The Egoist

in love with him as in love with love, and it is this false step, this mistaken engagement, which gives rise to the situation of the story.

The action of the story, from the seventh chapter onwards, takes place at Patterne Hall where Dr. Middleton and his daughter have been invited to stay for a month with Willoughby's aunts, the Ladies Eleanor and Isabel. Special attractions are held out for the Doctor in the shape of a wine-cellar, a library, and the company of Vernon Whitford, Willoughby's cousin and secretary. Clara is already beginning to criticise her lover's preoccupation with himself and to ponder whether she cannot retrieve the mistake of her engagement. She chafes at the lordly selfishness even of his generosity, wondering whether an escape is not yet possible with honour from a marriage which she has come to anticipate as the state "of a woman tied not to a man of heart, but to an obelisk lettered all over with hieroglyphics, and everlastingly hearing him expound them, relishingly renewing his lectures on them."*

* In ch. x Sir Willoughby actually supplies his own title, to Clara's amazement. He gravely warns her against marrying an egoist! This is a spurt of Meredith's fun.

George Meredith

Besides the sense of honour, however, Clara is fettered by a feeling of cowardice or impotence (see ch. xxv). She has no Harry Oxford to carry her off, for although Vernon Whitford and she have begun to admire each other, he is too loyal to make any move. He reads her, and she knows it, but his stedfast-ness of honour and his humility keep him from any intrigue.

Poor Sir Willoughby is blissfully uncon-scious of all that is passing in her heart. "The love-season is the carnival of egoism," and the fatuous baronet imagines that Clara shares the blind devotion to himself which inspires his aunts and Lætitia Dale.* His treatment of his dependents and his conversa-tion, revolving round the "I" of his worshipful and weariful personality, become more and more intolerable to his betrothed. Her first attempt to win liberty leads her to suggest that Lætitia would make a better wife for him, but he perversely sets this down to feminine jealousy, and actually invites her

* "With ladies his aim was the Gallican courtier of any period from Louis Treize to Louis Quinze. He could dote on those who led him to talk in that character—backed by English solidity, you understand."

The Egoist

assistance to marry off Lætitia to Vernon. Clara confides in Vernon, from whom she receives sensible, dispassionate advice, and also in Lætitia, who is amazed and horrified that any woman should propose to break with Sir Willoughby. On both sides she is foiled.

Meantime, Colonel Horace de Craye arrives. He is to be the best man at the marriage. Like Clara, he has Irish blood in his veins, and the pair of them strike up a merry friendship. De Craye detects the chasm between the lovers, and his budding hopes of carrying off Clara rouse Sir Willoughby's temper. "Remember," says Meredith, "the poets upon Jealousy. It is to be haunted in the heaven of two by a Third." Willoughby is now beginning to be angry and seriously alarmed at the state of matters, while Clara, unable to persuade her father to leave the cellar and comforts of Patterne Hall, and too shrewd to rely on De Craye, determines to depart secretly. A series of accidents, however, forces her to return from the railway station, in the company of Colonel De Craye who has suspected her design. Sir Willoughby's wrath is

kindled at her deception and at her confidence
in the Colonel; besides, the rumour of Clara's
attempted flight has got abroad in the county,
and he has now to face the terror of being
twice jilted. His reputation is in jeopardy.
He philanders once more with Lætitia, in
order to have her in reserve, should the worst
come to the worst, while Clara confides in
Mrs. Mountstuart Jenkinson, the witty lady
of the district. Sir Willoughby feels he has
been betrayed, and his injured pride is up in
arms. The policy he sketches for himself is
to prevent De Craye at any cost from marrying Clara. He proposes to pair off Vernon and
Miss Middleton and to marry Lætitia himself, so as to be able to say that he generously
handed over Clara to his cousin and secretary,
"who opened his mouth and shut his eyes,"
while he himself remained true to "the lady
of his first and strongest affections." Poor
gentleman! He reckons confidently upon
Lætitia, who was always at his beck and call;
but, to his horror, she refuses the offer of his
hand. To be pitied by her is bad; to be
rejected by her is fearful! In terror of being
left brideless, and exposed to the jeers of a

The Egoist

world which he affected to despise, he puts
fresh pressure on Clara, who hears indirectly
of his secret proposal to Lætitia and taxes him
roundly with a breach of faith which condones
her refusal to abide by the engagement. Sir
Willoughby, driven to his wits' end, pretends
he has been proposing to Lætitia on Vernon's
behalf, and meantime makes a last desperate
effort to save his vanity from the gossip
and ridicule of the county.* Vernon and
Clara own tentatively and tenderly to one
another the love which has been ripening
slowly out of their friendship. But Sir
Willoughby has to rave in a persistent and
unmanly fashion, employing all manner of
artifices and arguments, before he can induce
the disillusioned Lætitia to accept his hand.
She tells him and his aunts frankly that she
will try to respect him, but that she cannot
venerate him, much less love a "gentleman
nurtured in idolatry." Sir Willoughby, however, is only too glad to take her on these terms,
and the curtain falls upon Vernon and Clara together as the true lovers, while the poor Egoist
is mated to a woman who heartily despises him.

* Compare Alvan's horror at the thought of being jilted, in "The Tragic
Comedians" (ch. xiv).

George Meredith

Both Lætitia* and Clara avow themselves to be egoists, but neither deserves the title in the sense in which Sir Willoughby earns it. Meredith indeed never drew a female Egoist. Religion and love are the two phases of experience where a human being is most apt to be engrossed with himself. "A man," says Tolstoy in "The Cossacks," "is never so much an egotist as at the moment when his whole being is stirred with spiritual exaltation. It seems to him that there is nothing in the world more beautiful, more interesting, than himself at such a moment." But Meredith eschews this line of analysis. Only in "Queen Theodolinda" and in one or two casual allusions does he touch upon the danger of self-engrossment in the sphere of personal religion. Love, on the other hand, furnishes him with rich material for the study of egoism, and, as the male has usually more initiative and scope in love than the woman, this is probably one reason why Sir Willoughby remains without any female counterpart in his

* Lily Dale, the jilted heroine whose woes had moved the readers of "The Small House at Allington," fifteen years before, is not given the chance of action at the close which Meredith confers on Lætitia Dale, and in any case she is as water unto wine compared with the later Miss Dale.

266

gallery of portraits. The baronet is a blend of pride and sentimentalism. The lover as sentimentalist had been already drawn at full length in Wilfrid Pole, as well as in his sister Cornelia and her lover. But Sir Willoughby answers to Peacock's definition of "Sentiment," in his pessimistic essay upon "The Four Ages of Poetry," as "canting egotism in the mask of refined feeling," and Meredith has treated him with the severity and sparkle of the true Comic Spirit. He is not drawn with satirical irony. The author plays with him, draws him out in his strong points as well as in his foibles, and punishes him with such dexterity as almost to blind the reader to his sorry fate. Hardly anyone who reads the book for the first time fails to wish that Sir Willoughby had not succeeded in protecting himself against the gossip of the county. He seems to get off too easily. We wish Lætitia had held her ground. But when one reflects that he has to marry a woman *

* It is part of Meredith's triumph not only to have depicted Lætitia and Clara as loyal to one another, in spite of their relations to Sir Willoughby, but to have drawn Lætitia without awakening a suspicion of ridicule. The woman, whose love has been trifled with, remains a dignified figure ; she never descends to be spiteful or resentful.

George Meredith

who has seen through him, a former adorer
who has turned critic and judge, and that—
instead of tossing his glove for her to pick up
humbly—he has had to woo her in sheer
desperation, then one begins to understand
the deadly significance of the last sentence in
the book. Stevenson wrote of it: "here is a
Nathan for the modern David; here is a
book to send the blood into men's faces . . .
It is yourself that is hunted down; these are
your faults that are dragged into the day, and
numbered, with lingering relish, with cruel
cunning and precision. A young friend of
Mr. Meredith's (as I have heard the story)
came to him in an agony. 'This is too bad of
you,' he cried. 'Willoughby is me.' 'No,
my dear fellow,' said the author; 'he is all of
us.' I have read 'The Egoist' five or six
times myself, and I mean to read it again; for
I am like the young friend of the anecdote—I
think Willoughby an unmanly but a very
serviceable exposure of myself."

To Lætitia Meredith is more tender than to
almost any other of his prominent feminine
characters, for Dorothy Beltham is always in
the shade, like Clare Doria Forey. If she is

The Egoist

the victim of the Egoist's callousness,* she
gets her revenge heaped up and brimming
over in the end. Clara, the "dainty rogue
in porcelain," has neither the wit nor the
courage of her sisters in the front rank of
Meredith's heroines—Aminta Farrell or
rather Clotilde is perhaps nearest to her in
general character—but she has more charm
and warmth than some of them, just because
she is cast upon a less heroic scale.

The minor characters of the book need
little or no comment. In "Mansfield Park"
the daughter of a marine is adopted by her
aristocratic relatives, but in "The Egoist" it
is a boy—Crossjay—one of the most natural
and delightful lads in all the novels. Every
line about Crossjay tells. "It was a good
month before he could see pudding taken
away from table without a sigh of regret that
he could not finish it as deputy for the Devon-
port household. . . . He was not only
indolent, he was opposed to the acquisition
of knowledge through the medium of books,

---

* " Men who are Egoists have *good* women for their victims; women on
whose devoted constancy they feed; they drink it like blood." This
remark of Clara helps to open Lætitia's eyes. It shows that Thackeray's
Arthur Pendennis was not quite an Egoist of the Meredithian type.

George Meredith

and would say: 'But I don't want to!' in a tone to make a logician thoughtful." Some traits in the character of Vernon Whitford, "a Phœbus Apollo turned friar," are supposed to have been drawn from Sir Leslie Stephen, but he is of the same fibre as Redworth, and Dr. Middleton's indifference to his daughter's matrimonial difficulties is a replica of General Ople's attitude towards Elizabeth. The admission in the prelude that Egoism has a sober and serviceable and valiant phase in the upbuilding of social and national tenacity, is a brief echo of what Meredith had already explained in the second chapter of "Beauchamp's Career."

The novel is stronger in dialogue and analysis than in epigrams. Meredith has put some of his most original work into the vivid descriptive passages which occur in the accounts of "the aged and great wine" (ch. xx)—an admirable mock-heroic study—, the rain-storm (ch. xxvi), the conversation at lunch (ch. xxxvi), and, on a smaller scale, Clara's beauty (in chapters v and ix and xviii). The brilliant prelude, with its sough of Carlyle, is spoiled by the dreadful

The Egoist

Meredithese which recurs here and there throughout the later chapters, but it is a fitting pendant to "The Essay on Comedy," and serves as an introduction to more than one of the major novels. An equally characteristic passage occurs at the end of ch. xxxvi, where, after the conversation at lunch, Lady Culmer admits to Sir Willoughby, "Though what it all meant, and what was the drift of it, I couldn't tell to save my life. Is it every day the same with you here?" "Very much." "How you must enjoy a spell of dulness!" This is a remark which comes home to the reader of some conversations in the next four novels. The dialogue flashes with crisp repartee and brilliant epigram, but now and then we do get the contortions of the Sibyl without her inspiration—partly owing to the fact that "The Egoist," especially in its latter half, is a study of misconceptions and cross-purposes. The treatment suits the subject, though the Comic Spirit has been infected with the affectation and trickery of its prey. There are deep things in the book, but here as in some of the ballads and larger poems you have not only to dive far down but to

George Meredith

wriggle through a mass of waving tangle under which the treasure has been hidden. Meredith here, even more than elsewhere, "delights in elaborate analysis of abstruse problems, whose solutions when reached are scarcely less difficult to ordinary apprehension than are the problems themselves; discriminating countless shades where the common eye sees but one gloom or glare; pursuing countless distinct movements where the common eye sees only a whirling perplexity." These words of James Thomson state the impression of Meredith's art with great precision, as it is revealed in "The Egoist." The development of the relations between Vernon and Clara, for example, is an illustration of the author's subtle diagnosis which is less poignant than his dissection of Cecilia's feelings toward Beauchamp but which was hardly bettered till he came to weigh the quivering, netted soul of Nataly Radnor. The essence of the art, however, does not lie in the fact that the author enters into the inner feelings of the characters, instead of describing them from the standpoint of an outsider. That would simply be dramatic

The Egoist

skill. What he does is to analyse motives of which often the actors, no less than the on-lookers, are almost unconscious. It is this feature which is responsible for the delicacy as well as for the persistent unreality felt by the reader of the novels, and which has helped to make the latter half of "The Egoist" caviare to the general.

THE TRAGIC COMEDIANS

The Tragic Comedians

THE sub-title of this novel is "a study in a well-known story," *i.e.,* the tragic story of the final love-affair in the life of Ferdinand Lassalle, a brilliant young Jewish Hungarian, the leader of the German Republican Socialists, who died, after a meteoric career, on August 31st, 1864, from the effects of a duel. Sixteen years later Meredith's book appeared. It sits close to the facts of the story. Nothing in it is invented, "because an addition of fictitious incidents could never tell us how she came to do this, he to do that; or how the comic in their natures led by interplay to the tragic issue." The novel is an actual transcript of "the bare railway line of their story," and though it is set out with all the intellectual power and ethical insight which the writer's genius has at its command, this fidelity has handicapped the movement of his imagination. One advantage of it, however, is that the reader needs to know * nothing but the correspondence of the names. These are as follows:

Ferdinand Lassalle	Sigismund Alvan
Helene von Dönniges	Clotilde von Rüdiger
Yanko von Racowitza	Prince Marko Romaris
Baron Korff	Count Kollin
Countess von Hatzfeldt	Lucie, Baroness von Crefeldt
Rustow	Tresten
Dr. Haenle	Dr. Störchel

Clotilde, a young German beauty, has had two love-affairs before she meets with Alvan. Her first lover, Count Constantine, was flung over for the dashing young Prince Marko Romaris. But even the latter failed to satisfy her heart. Her sentimental dream was not of an adoring pliant fiancé but, like Margarita in "Farina," she expected a Siegfried who would dominate her by sheer superiority and force of character. For Clotilde, as Meredith

* To the third edition, revised by the author and published by Messrs. Ward, Lock, Bowden, and Co., in 1892, Mr. Clement Shorter prefixed an adequate statement of the historical basis underlying the novel.

The Tragic Comedians

draws her, is one of the revolutionary aristo-crats. Her parents and circle belong to the class of established conservatives ; her father is a gouty old Bavarian diplomatist, her mother a faded beauty of Society, but she herself is a vivid aspiring young woman whose ideal of manhood is higher than any men known to her. She dreams of some eagle, some predestined mate. Only, "the man must be a gentleman. Poets, princes, war-riors, potentates, marched before her speculative fancy unselected." *

It is in this receptive mood that she first hears of Alvan, when she is nineteen and he is thirty-nine. She is told that she resembles Alvan in her talk, but that Alvan is no gentleman, only a diabolically clever Jew and a notorious demagogue, who by birth and position is utterly antagonistic to all her inherited instincts. The girl's curiosity is whetted. The two meet at a party in Berlin, and at once fall in love with each other.

* Compare the similar dream of the sentimental Cornelia Pole in "Sandra Belloni" (ch. i), whose " heart of hearts demanded for her as spouse, a lord, a philosopher, and a Christian, in one ; and he must be a Member of Parliament. Hence her isolated air." Both women found the issue of their love-episodes to be tragic.

George Meredith

The infatuation is sudden and complete on both sides. For he too confesses he had heard of her as "a gold-crested serpent," just when he was in lack of a comrade. "I wanted my comrade young and fair, necessarily of your sex, but with heart and brain : an insane request, I fancied, until I heard that you were the person I wanted." Their common anticipations and aspirations burst through all conventions at this interview. Alvan escorts her home and prepares to surmount the social barriers that lie between him and her family. The girl's heart fails her for a moment at the thought of her relatives' horror over Alvan's "hissing reputation—for it was a reputation that stirred the snakes and the geese of the world." But his overwhelming passion carries her away. The two go through "a demi-ceremony of betrothal." Then Clotilde is ordered to Switzerland for her health, whither Alvan also retires after a successful political campaign. The two meet once more, this time at Berne, and the struggle begins between Clotilde's *bourgeois* prejudices and conventional instincts on the one side and on the other the passion kindled

The Tragic Comedians

in her by Alvan's hot wooing.* The latter
urges an immediate elopement. But Clotilde
hesitates to cast the die for love, although he
removes one obstacle, viz., the prejudice
excited by his previous connexion with an
older married woman, the Baroness von
Crefeldt, whose cause he had chivalrously
championed, though at the cost of stirring
considerable scandal round his own name.

The two at last part on the understanding
that Alvan is to see her parents formally next
day at Geneva. But the crisis comes otherwise. Clotilde, on breaking the news to her
family, is appalled at their brutal wrath and
the curses heaped upon her lover ; she flies
to throw herself upon his protection, and is
now prepared to do what he had urged some
days before. The girl's passion has risen over
the barriers of social convention ; she is ready
and eager to elope. Unluckily Alvan
hesitates. Too sure of his ability to overcome
her parents' opposition, driven by a certain
pride to the resolve that he would have no

* With Alvan's inability to understand women ("women for him were
objects to be chased, the politician's relaxation," ch. vii) compare the
similarly tragic misunderstanding of woman's character cherished by Carlo
Ammiani in " Vittoria " (ch. xli).

run-away bride, and also fearing to hurt the socialist cause by any scandal, he dissuades Clotilde from her proposal and hands her back to her family, bidding her leave the rest of the fighting to himself. His mistimed prudence and mixture of conceit and chivalry are his undoing. To the stunned girl it seems as if he had tossed her off and rejected her self-sacrifice. Abandoned by her lover she finds herself exposed to furious pressure from her scandalised relatives and at last she submits to their entreaties.

Meanwhile Alvan plots and chafes within the false position into which his pride had flung him. "Ceasing to be a social rebel, he conceived himself as a recognised dignitary, and he passed under the bondage of that position." Now he sees, too late, that he had cringed to the world instead of, as usual, defying it, when he resolved to let Clotilde go. The latter is removed from the town, out of reach of Alvan's machinations. His letters never reach her. Even his envoys, distrustful of their leader's alliance with a daughter of Society, mislead Clotilde, who finally is forced to write and sign a letter to Alvan

282

closing their connexion by announcing her engagement to Prince Marko. Thus her family's diplomacy triumphs, the more so that it is abetted secretly by Alvan's friends who disapprove of their leader's marriage. Clotilde believes she is deserted by Alvan for his former flame, the Baroness, while he in a fury of rage believes that Clotilde has perjured herself. Driven desperate, she declines, to Alvan's treacherous envoy, a final interview with Alvan himself. The latter, provoked beyond control, challenges her father to a duel. Prince Marko undertakes the challenge, and—to the surprise of all, and the bitter disappointment of Clotilde, who secretly hopes for another issue—Alvan falls. Three days later he is dead. Clotilde then marries Marko, who dies a few months afterwards. "From that day, or it may be, on her marriage day, her heart was Alvan's."

Though the frame-work of the story is borrowed, Meredith has enriched it with some of his most brilliant and original aphorisms. "Barriers are for those who cannot fly." "Try to think individually upon what you have to learn collectively—that is your

283

task." "It is the soul that does things in thi life—the rest is vapour." "The choicest women are those who yield not a feather of their womanliness for some amount of man-like strength." "Harness is harness, and a light yoke-fellow can make a proud career deviate." The wine-chapter or rapture, which Meredith must have in almost every one of his novels, occurs in ch. iv. Apart from this, the most prominent passages in the book are the allusions to Hamlet (ch. iii—iv), the glow-ing defence of light literature in ch. vi (while in the following chapter we seem to hear Meredith himself speaking through the words—"My pen is my fountain—the key of me ; and I give myself, I do not sell. I write when I have matter in me and in the direction it presses for, otherwise not a word"), the sketch of Bismarck in ch. vii, the outburst against Horace (the piper of the bourgeois in soul") in ch. xiv, and the vindication of idealism (in ch. xv, as already in chs. xv—xvi of "Vittoria ").

There are three ominous hints of the coming tragedy thrown out as the novel proceeds. One is the title of "Indian Bacchus" applied to Prince Marko, whose ultimate rôle it is to console this forlorn Ariadne after her nobler Theseus has gone.* Another is the blighted black lihcen-smitten tree (ch. vii), which the lovers pass and repass near Berne. The third is Alvan's musing remark in their first conversation : "Part of you may be shifty sand. The sands are famous for their golden shining —as you shine. Well, then, we must make the quicksands concrete" (ch. iv). Set this beside the remark in ch. ix: "he, when no longer flattered by the evidence of his mastery, took her for sand"—and you have the clue to Meredith's treatment of the whole affair between the two lovers. It is his favourite topic, the thwarting power of conventional society, especially with regard to women, who are daughters of the Philistines, and rarely possess sufficient courage to be true to themselves. That was Clotilde's weakness. Her training and situation were against bravery. Alvan saw that before she did (see ch. vi), and the tragedy of the situation was that when she came to recognise this, false pride

* This recalls one of Diana's witticisms (see the opening chapter of "Diana of the Crossways ").

prevented him from taking her at her word. Society is thus to blame for such a tragedy. So is the woman herself, however. And so is the man.

Alvan is represented as a tragic comedian, "that is, a grand self-pretender, a self-deceiver." Meredith interprets his character as a fine mind wrecked by stormy blood. He was "a revolutionist in imagination, the workman's friend in rational sympathy, their leader upon mathematical calculation, but a lawyer, a reasoner in law, and therefore of necessity a cousin germane, leaning to become an ally, of the Philistines." Thus his passion for a daughter of the Philistines might, if successful, have meant the blunting of his radical edge. As a matter of fact, his momentary deference to Philistine sentiment in his courtship proved his ruin. He ceased to be himself. He was no longer independent of opinion and single-minded, and he paid for the lapse into vanity.

Like Sir Willoughby Patterne, Alvan is an egoist, who has a fear of being jilted, for jilting means ridicule ; he also seeks to master for his own purposes the mind of a young lady

The Tragic Comedians

whose heart he has captured. "When we are man and wife," he boasts, "then I shall have 'will' enough for both, and she will be as clay in the hands of the potter." "It is really a piece of extraordinary good fortune that at the age of thirty-nine and a half, I should be fortunate enough to find a wife so beautiful, so sympathetic—who loves me so much, and who—an indispensable requirement—is so entirely absorbed in my personality." What is pure comedy in the Mr. Collins of "Pride and Prejudice" becomes tragedy in the pages of Meredith's semi-historical romance.

DIANA OF THE CROSSWAYS

Diana of the Crossways

THIS novel, issued in book-form in 1885, had a larger immediate success than any other of Meredith's romances; it went through no fewer than three editions in the year of publication. There was a special reason for this. "Diana" was published in a time of political excitement, and it carried on the political motive which had been operative in the previous two or three novels. It proved to be more significant as the first of the final quartette which were all to handle with some daring the problems of modern marriage, but what helped largely to recommend it to the public, was its reputation as a *roman à clef*.* Like its immediate predecessor, it drew upon a

---

* The facts were summarised in an article which appeared in "Temple Bar," vol. cxxi. The colourless notes written by Lord Melbourne, which the Hon. George Norton actually produced as evidence, are said to have supplied a hint to Dickens when he was writing the famous trial-scene in Pickwick.

comparatively recent episode which had
caused a huge sensation in political circles,
though Meredith's use of the radiant and
witty Caroline Norton's career was far more
free and slight and kind than his treatment
of Helene von Dönniges. In "The Tragic
Comedians" he had laced his philosophy on the
woman's version of a love-episode in her life.
His sympathy with Lassalle had made him
unjust to Helene, and therefore inartistic; the
attempt to gloss over the dismal stupidity of
the hero's attempt to find a Republican
princess in a sweet, forward, weak coquette,
left the latter unequal to the weight of the
dramatic situation. In "Diana," however,
Meredith was in love with his heroine, and
the husband of real life offered no serious
obstacle to the novelist's art. The result was
a masterpiece, which has had far more than
an ephemeral or factitious success.

Diana Antonia Merion is a clever and
beautiful young Irish orphan,* whose closest
friend is Lady Dunstane. "I nursed her,"
says the latter, "when she was an infant; my

---

* Like Aminta, Diana has also a vein of Spanish blood in her.

Diana of the Crossways

father and Dan Merion were chums. We
were parted by my marriage and the voyage
to India." When the story opens, Sir Lukin,
Lady Dunstane's husband, is retiring from the
army for the ostensible reason of looking after
his estates at Copsley in Surrey and in Scot-
land, and of devoting himself to his wife, whose
health is not strong. Lady Dunstane meets
Diana once more at a Dublin ball, given in
honour of an Irish general.* The girl is
nineteen and alone in the world ; during a
series of visits to various country-houses in
England she finds her unprotected position is
rendered intolerable by the odious attentions
of certain male guests. She returns to
Copsley, where she imagines she is safe with
her friend. To her horror, however, she
discovers that Sir Lukin is trying to take
liberties with her. In order to spare Emma,
her friend, she keeps silence upon the insult.
But her outraged pride and sense of loyalty to
Lady Dunstane force her to the conviction
that Copsley cannot any longer be a real
home to her ; she departs on a round of visits,

* "She makes everything in the room dust round a blazing jewel," says
Lord Larrian.

293

and the next news of her is that she is to
marry a Mr. Augustus Warwick, aged thirty-
four, nearly fifteen years her senior. He is a
retired barrister, a cold, self-satisfied person,
whom Lady Dunstane compared to "a house
locked up and empty: a London house
conventionally furnished and decorated by
the upholsterer and empty of inhabitants."
Diana had once dubbed him "a gentlemanly
official"; she had met him first at the Crossways, of which his aunt and uncle were
tenants, and her reason for marrying him is
attributed by Meredith mainly to an impulse
of self-defence. She is not in love with him.
She simply wants a husband in order to secure
a position in the social world which will
relieve her from unpleasant attentions. The
dismay of Lady Dunstane—who is baffled by
Diana's action—is only equalled by the
disappointment of Mr. Thomas Redworth, a
sterling gentleman,* who had been in love
with the brilliant beauty since the night of the

* In ch. v Meredith, by one of his flying touches, notes Redworth's
appreciation of Diana's mind as well as of her beauty. "Her view of things
had a throne beside his own, even in their differences." Add the fine
passage in ch. xxxvii: "Redworth believed in the soul of Diana. . . She was
a soul; therefore perpetually pointing to growth in purification," etc.

Diana of the Crossways

Irish ball but had hesitated to propose to her on account of an honourable conviction that no man has the right to court a woman unless he has bank-book ability to support her comfortably. Redworth's financial position, however, has improved so much that he is on the point of asking Diana's hand, when the news of her mysterious engagement arrives. He is too staunch and brave to be piqued. He magnanimously wishes Diana to know "she has not lost a single friend through her marriage."

The girl soon needs all her friends. Before long she realises that her marriage has been a alse step. She and her husband are hopelessly incompatible. Her house in England is called "The Crossways," and the name becomes grimly symbolic of her situation. "No two," she confesses, "ever came together so naturally antagonistic as we two. We walked a dozen steps in stupefied union, and hit upon crossways. From that moment it was tug and tug; he me, and I him. By resisting, I made him a tyrant, and he by insisting made me a rebel." Her husband's ambitions bring them into political society, where Diana, in reckless indifference to gossip, soon enters

George Meredith

upon an apparently compromising relationship with the Whig premier, Lord Dannisburgh. Her rôle is that of his Egeria. She finds in him what she misses in her husband, appreciation of her wit and intelligence. Warwick, in a fit of malign jealousy, sues for a divorce. Diana, proudly conscious of her innocence but shrinking from a public scandal, which would oblige her to act the part of injured innocent, prepares to leave England. Lady Dunstane, feeling that this would expose her to fatal misconception, sends Redworth to intercept her. He finds her at "The Cross-ways" and, after a great scene—one of the strong passages in the book—induces her to return first to Copsley and then to London, where her friends rally round her. The case is decided in her favour (rather to her secret disappointment), but she has soon to be taken abroad by friends in order "to escape the meshes of the terrific net of the marital law, brutally whirled to capture her by the man her husband." The sick, jealous partner in the background, trying to thwart a mate in the open, is a foretaste of Mrs. Burman in "One of Our Conquerors."

296

Diana of the Crossways

This is the first phase of Diana's married life. The second opens with her literary ambitions. She takes to writing fiction, partly for the sake of a livelihood, and returns to London to enter on the career of a successful novelist and a society lady with a *salon* or circle of congenial spirits. Meantime, however, she has met * and fascinated † the Hon. Percy Dacier, Lord Dannisburgh's nephew, who is a rising young politician; her second novel, "The Young Minister of State," is supposed to be a study of him, and gossip is rife upon their relationship, which is in reality ripening into a genuine love-passion. Mr. Warwick's renewed threats of enforcing his marital rights bring matters to a head.‡ Dacier pleads with her to elope with him. In desperation she eventually consents, but, on the eve of departing, she is summoned to Copsley where Lady Dunstane has to undergo

---

* The description of this meeting, at Rovio, in ch. xvi, is a fresh illusrtation of Meredith's ability to set nature and human moods in rhythm.

† The rather melodramatic episode of her vigil beside the corpse of the Prime Minister heightens the emotional tension between her and Dacier.

‡ The scene between Diana and Lady Watkin (in ch. xxiii) recalls the inimitable interview between Célimène and Arsinoé in the fourth scene of the third act of "Le Misanthrope"—one of Meredith's favourite comedies (alluded to in ch. xviii).

a serious operation. Redworth is her lady-ship's messenger, and thus he again intervenes —this time unconsciously—so as to save Diana from a false step. "I am always at Crossways," she reflects, "and he saves me."

Nearly a year passes before Dacier and Diana meet again. The former has got over the blow to his pride inflicted by Diana's failure to keep her promise, and their passion is renewed. What finally wrecks it is Diana's betrayal of a political secret which he entrusted to her. She tells this to the editor of "The Times"; Dacier angrily throws her off, and the next news of him is his engagement to a Miss Constance Asper, with whom his name had been connected for some years. Diana collapses under the shock. Mr. Warwick dies, by the irony of events, but while she is now free to marry Dacier, the latter has broken with her. Lady Dunstane nurses her back to health and spirits, and eventually Redworth persuades her to accept his long-tried love. When she had begun life, she had undervalued his noble heart. "I wanted a hero, and the jewelled garb and the feather did not suit him." But she is now

Diana of the Crossways

cured of her girlish sentimentalism, which tended among other things to make her regard courage as essentially a military virtue (compare the thirty-first chapter of "Beauchamp's Career"). Her wounded pride takes longer to heal. Not for some time does she consent, like Mrs. Millamant, to "dwindle into a wife." The treatment she has received during her married life makes her reluctant to give up her new liberty. "The thought of a husband cuts one from any dreaming. It's all dead flat earth at once!" (compare the outbursts in chs. iv and xiv). Thanks largely to Lady Dunstane's wise management, however, which recalls the treatment of Emilia by Powys and his sister, Diana ceases to be hyper-sensitive; she no longer shifts and winds to escape Redworth's patient wooing; and her hesitation at last yields to the chivalry and nobility of her lover. Lady Dunstane had stamped him as "one of those rare men of honour who can command their passion; who venerate when they love." Diana comes to recognise the truth of this characterisation before it is too late, and Meredith for once allows his readers to lay down a novel

George Meredith

with that sense of pleasure which Darwin thought every novel should provide at the close of its evolutions.

Later editions of "Diana" contain the following prefatory note. "A lady of high distinction for wit and beauty, the daughter of an illustrious Irish house, came under the shadow of calumny. It has latterly been examined and exposed as baseless. The story of 'Diana of the Crossways' is to be read as fiction." Thereby hangs a tale. Certain traits in Diana's character had been originally derived from that of Caroline Norton, the novelist. A granddaughter of Sheridan, who had married a barrister, the Hon. George Norton, she was the defendant in an unsuccessful divorce-case in which Lord Melbourne, the Prime Minister, appeared as co-respondent.* Mrs. Norton, who continued to live as a beautiful and popular woman in London society, was further suspected of having disclosed to the editor of the "Times" Sir Robert Peel's decision to

* Melbourne, then over fifty, was one of her admirers. She had applied to him, for the sake of his friendship with her father, to procure an appointment for her lazy husband.

repeal the Corn Laws, a secret which had been told her in confidence by Sidney Herbert, one of her admirers. Lord Dufferin subsequently found that this rumour was unfounded. The person responsible for the journalistic *coup* was Lord Aberdeen, and, so far from the transaction being surreptitious, it is probable that the communication was made with Sir Robert Peel's consent.

Meredith's analysis of the motives which led his Diana to take this step is the weak spot in the novel. If any explanation is to be sought for this inexplicable action, the real clue probably lies in her excited mood, when Dacier came back at night to tell her the great secret. "Her present mood was a craving for excitement—for incident, wild action." She could not satisfy this craving in the story she was writing, and when an opportunity of gratifying her passion for dramatic effect in real life came, it was the psychological moment.* The great editor had often taunted her with the staleness of her news. Now, she was a day or two before anyone, and she

* Dacier, for his own purpose, "had artfully lengthened out 'the news,' to excite and overbalance her."

301

leapt at the chance of astonishing her friend the journalist and of enjoying a thrilling moment of triumph. She was on the verge of bankruptcy, thanks to her extravagant mode of life,* but the price of the secret was not her primary motive. The curious thing is that she seems to have ignored any thought of an injury done to Dacier. The liberty he had taken of embracing her had evidently humiliated her pride and stirred a fit of resentment against him, which prevented her from considering his feelings. The result of the interview with the editor, Meredith is careful to explain, is to revive her sense of importance and self-esteem. It was not till the indignant Dacier taxed her next day with treachery, that the full meaning of her impulsive action broke upon her.

It was not only from Mrs. Norton, however, that Meredith drew the portrait of his Diana. One must also read, in this connexion, some sentences from his introduction to the new edition (1902) of "Lady Duff Gordon's

---

* She had fluttered into speculation in the city, like Lady Grace in "One of Our Conquerors," but there was no Mr. Radnor to pluck her out before she was plucked.

Diana of the Crossways

Letters from Egypt." "Women, not en-
thusiasts, inclined rather to criticise, and to
criticise so independent a member of their sex
particularly, have said that her entry into a
ball-room took the breath. Poetical compari-
sons run under heavy weights in prose ; but
it would seem, in truth, from the reports of
her, that wherever she appeared she could be
likened to Selene breaking through cloud ;
and, further, the splendid vessel was richly
freighted. Trained by a scholar, much in the
society of scholarly men, having an innate bent
to exactitude, and with a ready tongue docile
to the curb, she stepped into the world to be
a match for it. She cut her way through the
accustomed troop of adorers, like what you
will that is buoyant and swims gallantly."
This characterisation of a woman who combined radiant beauty * with a fine intelligence
suggests one of the quarters where Meredith
must have found hints not only for Clara
Middleton but for Diana Warwick.

Meredith compares her (in ch. viii) to
Hermione, who also was a beautiful wife

* The dark brows and Grecian features of Lady Gordon correspond to
what we are told of Diana's personal appearance in ch. i.

suspected and wronged by her vindictive husband. But Hermione was a mother; she became reconciled to Leontes in the end; and her love lacked any impulsive or ardent passion. In all these respects, particularly in the last, Diana differs from her Shakesperean prototype. What really suggests Hermione is the bravery and high spirits of Mrs. Warwick,* who also has the good fortune to enjoy the devoted confidence and respect of her supporters. Hermione is not witty, but Diana is given some of the author's happiest and deepest sayings. "The more I know of the world the more clearly I perceive that its top and bottom sin is cowardice, physically and morally alike." "We women miss life only when we have to confess we have never met the man to reverence." "Gossip is a beast of prey that does not wait for the death of the creature it devours." "We women are taken to be the second thoughts of the Creator; human nature's fringes, mere finish-

---

* Not invariably, of course. Meredith is too wise to make of her, any-more than of Vittoria, a plaster model. Compare her confession of vanity and cowardice in ch. xxvii and her sentimental worship of military courage at the outset. "I am open to be carried on a tide of unreasonableness when the coward cries out."

ing touches, not a part of the texture." "To be pointedly rational is a greater difficulty to me than a fine delirium." This last aphorism is taken from the opening chapter, which is of the same stuff as the preludes to "The Amazing Marriage" and "The Egoist," but the writing is more personal and less abstract than in the latter case. It is better read after than before a first perusal of the story. Meredith's triple object is to create an atmosphere of expectancy for the entrance of his heroine, to analyse sentimentalism afresh, and to defend his own method of philosophic fiction more widely and vigorously than in the introduction to "The Tragic Comedians." One of Diana's sayings quoted in this chapter, by the way, beginning: "A brown cone drops from the fir-tree before my window, a nibbled green from the squirrel. Service is our destiny in life and death"—is the prose core of the little "Dirge in the Woods" which he had written fourteen years before.* In the "nuptial chapter" which closes the

* Another saying on the world ("From the point of vision of the angels this ugly monster, only half out of slime, must appear our one constant hero") anticipates the thought of the lines on "Men and Man" which appeared two years later in "Ballads and Poems of Tragic Life."

novel, Diana returns to the same thought.
"Marriage," she reflects, "might be the arch-
way to the road of good service."

Lady Dunstane is a closer friend to Diana
than Rebecca Wythan to Carinthia, and Redworth's part * in her life is more intimate than
that of Owain Wythan, but Redworth is
moulded out of the same clay as the Welsh
squires in "Sandra Belloni" or in "The
Amazing Marriage," and, next to Dacier, this
staunch, humble, honourable admirer is the
most important male figure in Diana's story.
When the tale opens, he is in Ireland on
Government business ; he happens to meet
the young beauty at the ball, where he falls
in love with her at first sight ; but too scrupu-
lously he waits till his income, swollen by
successful railway speculations, is large
enough to give this matchless girl what he
considers that she deserves. Redworth is the

* Like Matey Weyburn, he is a cricketer and looks well in flannels (see
ch. xl). Compare Crossjay's attempt to explain Vernon Whitford's
reliable character to Clara (in "The Egoist," ch. viii). "If you look on at
cricket, in comes a safe man for ten runs. He may get more, and he never
gets less ; and you should hear the old farmers talk of him in the booth."
This is rather clever for a boy, but it hits off the class of men to whom
Redworth belongs (see above, page 42). He wins Diana for the reason
given by Faust : "Nur der verdient die Gunst der Frauen, der kräft'gst sie
zu schützen weiss."

Diana of the Crossways

high hero of the book, though he is an M.P., and Meredith honours him by putting into his lips the acute estimate of the Irish character in ch. iii ("Irishmen are, like horses, bundles of nerves; and you must manage them, as you do with all nervous creatures, with firmness but good temper, etc"). Next year the author interposed in the panic of the Home Rule controversy with four pages upon "Concessions to the Celt" (in the October "Fortnightly Review"), which appealed to the English public for sanity and justice instead of coercion. The article elaborated what the novel had suggested. One of its most characteristic passages is as follows: "The cries we have been hearing for Cromwell or for Bismarck prove the existence of an impatient faction in our midst fitter to wear the collars of those masters whom they invoke than to drop a vote into the ballot-box. . . . The braver exemplar for grappling with monstrous political tasks is Cavour, and he would not have hinted at the iron method or the bayonet for a pacification. Cavour challenged debate; he had faith in the active intellect, and that is the thing to be prayed for

George Meredith

by statesmen who would register permanent successes." Read with this the paragraphs in ch. xxi of the novel ; they reveal Meredith's possession of the "firm and instructed genius" which Bagehot happily ascribed to Scott in another province.

Diana's love of natural science (ch. xvi) reflects the teaching of "Melampus"; the same interest in botany, which was so vivid in Meredith's own mind, comes out in Selina Collett and Goren, amongst others. The book is also studded with little gems of woodland scenery, e.g., at the opening of ch. xix or of ch. xxxix. The latter passage characteristically describes how Diana felt her way back to mental peace and happiness by giving herself up to the habit of noting "what bird had piped, what flower was out on the banks, and the leaf of what tree it was that lay beneath the budding." It was her love of Nature that saved her from despair and cynicism.

ONE OF OUR CONQUERORS

One of Our Conquerors

THIS novel, published in book-form in 1891, received from most of its critics pail after pail of cold water. It is the least popular of all the novels, and this is due not simply to its subject—the union of a man and woman who defy the conventional marriage laws — but to its style and construction. The book has three supremely fine studies in character, Victor, Nataly, and Dudley Sowerby ; but, unluckily, it riots in Meredithese, and the sense of effort is more than the sense of power. Mr. William Watson, in his famous article in " The National Review" had asserted that no milder word than detestable could be applied to Meredith's style. Nothing but the blunt phrase of "intellectual coxcombry" could " adequately describe the airs of superiority, the affectation of originality, the sham profundities, the counterfeit subtleties, the

311

pseudo-oracularisms of this book." He was
alluding to "The Egoist," but his invective
applies more truly to "One of Our Conquerors."* It is blotted by ornate and forced
phrases, by a swarm of unusually recondite
allusions, and also by a singular weakness of
construction. Its pages are too crowded with
minor characters, who are rarely in proper
perspective, and of these the musical circle
which surrounds the Radnors is simply a
bundle of eccentricities labelled with names.
The sole exceptions are the Frenchwoman,
Mdlle. Louise de Seilles, and the ponderous
cleric, Septimus Barmby ; the former gets
the cosmopolitan comments on British insularity which Meredith loves to introduce,
while the latter is at least more human than
the rest of his brethren in this or in the other
novels, and is treated with a certain touch of
respect and even sympathy. The unusual
prominence given to the clergy among the
minor *dramatis personæ* is due to the fact that
the clergy, together with the lawyers, represent to Meredith the buttresses of the

* Célimène's remark on Damis applies to Meredith's style here :
"Il est guindé sans cesse ; et dans tous ses propos
On voit qu'il se travaille à dire les bons mots. "

conventional society, with its institutions and traditions, which the novelist is bent on criticising. Thus, while Peacock in his stories usually makes the Tory clerical *bon vivants* the exponents of his own philosophy of jovial delight in the good things of this world, Meredith turns upon them with caustic and even satirical contempt. From the priest in "Vittoria" to the cleric here, they exercise no influence whatever upon the central figures of the story. The Comic Spirit never penetrated into the inner world of vital Christianity, any more than Balzac's genius did.

The reader is tantalised all through the novel by references to an Idea which is supposed to elude Victor from beginning to end. No novel by a first-rate writer ever began worse, and this Idea is one of its mistakes. But an equally exasperating feature is the number of clever, nimble-witted digressions. Several of Meredith's novels tempt more than the hazy, lazy reader to repeat Don Quixote's advice to the puppet-showman: "Go straight on with your story, and don't run into curves and slants." "One of Our Conquerors" provokes this retort perhaps more often than any of its predecessors. Meredith loiters in it, and the loitering is all the more unsatisfactory that it is a pleasure to himself; it allows him to show off his psychological paces and to curvet from side to side of the road.

The main track of the tale is as follows.

Victor Montgomery Radnor, when barely twenty-one had married a middle-aged widow, Mrs. Burman, for the sake of her money. She was about forty years old and was enamoured of the gay, mercurial youth. She actually encouraged her young husband to practise singing along with her handsome lady-companion, a Miss Natalia Dreighton, the daughter of a good Yorkshire family. The two young people, thus thrown together, fell in love. Victor's inflammable nature started into rebellion against the false position in which he had placed himself; Nataly gave up the stage in order to save him from despair and worse, and the pair eloped. The first error of Victor's life had been submission to the world, a consent to secure wealth and social position at the expense of natural affection. He then tried to retrieve this error by breaking through the conventional limits of the world and following for the first time the instincts of Nature in the guise of love for Miss Dreighton.   Neither he nor Nataly ever regretted the step.*   Their marriage was perfectly happy ; a daughter Nesta was born to them ; and¦ Mr. Radnor amassed a large fortune in the City.   He was liberal and popular, desirous to be on good terms with all and sundry.   "Mr. Radnor could rationally say that he was made for happiness ; he flew to it, he breathed, he dispensed it."

To the world the pair seemed an ordinary husband and wife.   But their union was still illegal.   Mrs. Burman, instead of suing for a divorce, against which she had religious scruples, had preferred the subtler revenge of retaining her legal position as Radnor's wife, and thereby preventing him from marrying Natalia.   She had fallen into ill-health and never went into society.   No persecution of

---

* See the passage in ch. vi, the first of the marvellous analyses of Nataly's nature :—"Her surrender then might be likened to the detachment of a flower on the river's bank by swell of flood : she had no longer root of her own ; away she sailed, through beautiful scenery, with occasionally a crashing fall, a turmoil, emergence from a vortex, and once more the whirling surface. . . . But even when it is driving us on the breakers, call it love : and be not unworthy of it, hold to it." See further, ch. xi and ch. xxv.

the pair was undertaken by her. So long as they lived quietly, she never interfered. But the irrepressible social ambitions of Victor could not be satisfied short of an open and popular position in society,* and, whenever he made any such move, Mrs. Burman contrived to circulate rumours which let a cold wind of suspicion blow upon the pair, until they were obliged to withdraw. This had happened twice, at Craye Farm and Creckholt, where the situation had become intolerable for them, and especially for the sensitive Natalia. Mr. Radnor could not bear to stay where she had felt wounded by social ostracism. But, in spite of all this, he could not grasp the idea of a life simply lived according to Nature ; though his relations with Nataly had given him the chance of that, he madly tried to improve upon it by incongruously demanding the sanctions and luxuries of conventional society.

Victor, however, true to his name, has deter-

---

* It is characteristic of his inveterate sanguineness that he had been influenced, if not prompted, to this course of action by realising that he could exact respect from his partner and his partner's wife ; both of them knew the secret, and yet they were subservient to him. "Why," Victor argued, "this foreshadows a conquered world! If I can win them, I can win all the rest!"

316

mined to make a third and final effort to win the esteem of the world which he has defied. This is the second and tragic folly of his career. "A position secretly rebellious," Meredith explains, "is equal to water on the brain for stultifying us." He tries to keep from his wife and daughter the fact that he has bought a new estate and built a large mansion, to form the scene of fresh operations. There are special reasons for this move. Nesta is by this time nearly twenty-one, and for her sake especially the father feels that he must retrieve his false position before the world. There is a rumour, too, that Mrs. Burman is about to sue for a divorce at last. Altogether Victor is in his element, plotting for social happiness anew.

The book opens on the eve of the visit which he has arranged for his wife and daughter and a party of their friends to pay to Lakelands, by way of inaugurating the new venture. Nataly is alarmed and distressed at her husband's fresh infatuation. "Now once more they were to run the same round of alarms, undergo the love of the place, with perpetual apprehensions of having to leave it." Victor is even contemplating a seat in

317

George Meredith

Parliament, which, as she realises, will mean the exposure of herself and him and their daughter to the gossip of the world. She has no heart for her position of rebel against the world's conventions. But her love for Victor is genuine, and she is prepared as usual to let him have his way. The situation is complicated by Nesta, however. The daughter knows nothing of her parents' past. Neither does Dudley Sowerby, a young aristocrat,* who is courting Nesta with the full consent of Victor ; the latter sees in such a marriage the protection of his dear daughter, but Nataly honourably shrinks from allowing the youth to entangle himself unawares. Victor feels Nataly's lack of cordiality in the matter of Lakelands and of the love-suit ; he rather resents it and attributes it to a feminine lack of nerve. In reality her moral courage is greater than her physical ; the strain has produced symptoms of heart disease, and attacks of this illness periodically recur, although she conceals them heroically from her husband.

* Meredith's analysis of this young man's victory over pride and prejudice, through his love for Nesta, is one of the triumphs of the book. He develops from a cold, conventional scion of the Philistines into a manly fellow.

One of Our Conquerors

Meantime the campaign at Lakelands opens with great éclat, but Mrs. Burman once more interferes, by sending her butler to warn Victor that he must retire into obscurity. He, buoyed up by reports of her increasing ill-health, determines to defy her, and summons poor Nataly to face the risk of becoming Godiva to the gossips for a while. In order to prevent Nesta from hearing too much, he induces his two maiden sisters * near Tunbridge Wells to take her for a visit. As Sowerby's family-seat is in the neighbourhood, he uses his opportunity to woo Nesta successfully. Meantime the father and mother had fled to the Continent, to escape rumours about their position which were circulating round Lakelands.

Nataly, on her return, hears that Captain Dartrey Fenellan, a friend who has returned from South Africa, is now a widower, and conscious that he is a truer mate for Nesta than Sowerby, as well as sensible of her duty to the latter suitor, she takes her courage in her two hands and tells Sowerby the

* They are puritanic in their conventional horror of Victor's relation to Nataly, and it is only after persistent appeals (described with a farcical humour) that they consent to receive even Nesta.

relations between herself and Victor. The latter, who hears nothing about this step for a week, then feels slightly aggrieved at what he considers the lack of true courage on Nataly's part, whom he actually thinks inferior to a Lady Halley in this respect. He had wanted to wait till Mrs. Burman's death—which he confidently expected very soon—before speaking out. Meantime Nesta,* who has accompanied the Duvidney ladies to Brighton,† happens to meet a certain Mrs. Judith Marsett, who is one of the Rahabs of Society (compare the poem, "The Sage Enamoured and the Honest Lady"), but who is more wronged than evil. Nesta, with quick intuition, divines the good element in her and, in spite of a maidenly aversion, sympathises with her freely. Major Worrell, an objectionable friend of Mrs. Marsett, takes

---

* It is owing to Nesta's sisterly championship of Judith Marsett that Captain Marsett agrees to marry the woman who as yet has no legal title to his name.

† She had been entrusted to their care, to be out of harm's way. But it is when with them that she gets her eyes opened to the inner facts about women and men who are outside the laws of matrimony. When the good ladies arrange for her departure, they do so saying, "The good innocent girl we received from the hands of your father, we return to him; we are sure of that." But Nesta's visit to Brighton had changed her outlook upon life.

advantage of the girl's friendship with the latter to insult Nesta; for which Captain Dartrey Fenellan horsewhips him. The news of this scandal repels Sowerby; he has just managed to overcome his pride enough to go on with his engagement to Nesta, but this entanglement of her with a public scandal makes him inclined in a fit of disgust to give her up altogether. She, the last of all women to allow herself to be talked about, had become a topic at the clubs! Nesta, knowing nothing of this, goes home, and learns the secret of her birth from Nataly, whose heroism touches her heart. Mother and daughter at last fully understand one another. Victor, meanwhile, perseveres with his social campaign, which causes torture to the wife and the daughter; and, to make matters worse, Sowerby tells Nataly of the scandal round Nesta's name at Brighton. The mother is upset. She feels humiliated and irritated at the girl, fearing "that corruption must come of the contact with impurity." Their confidence is broken. Captain Dartrey reassures her, however; Nesta's conduct only adds to his admiration for the tall, pure-

George Meredith

minded girl, who had lifted Mrs. Marsett by her innocent sympathy. But Nataly refuses to be comforted. She now thinks Sowerby a more suitable husband for her daughter, whose indiscretion shows that she requires "for her husband a man whose character and station guaranteed protection instead of inciting to rebellion." Dartrey's character, on the contrary, appeals more and more to Nesta's growing sense of what a true mate must be in life, for the Captain takes an independent, unconventional view of women's rights. She resents Sowerby's plea that she should dissociate herself from a notorious woman, and, to the intense disappointment of her father and mother, decides to reject him. Victor had always associated Lakelands with her marriage to Sowerby, and the break-down of the latter project threatens to affect the former enterprise. He is undaunted, however, in his efforts to win a seat in Parliament. On the day before his candidature opens, he is summoned by Mrs. Burman, now on her death-bed, to an interview. Nataly accompanies him, and the dying woman formally forgives the pair. Victor's triumph

now seems at last within reach.* Mrs.
Burman's death will enable him to legalise
his union with Nataly; another week will
see them settled in Lakelands; and a seat
in Parliament will crown his social ambitions. But the strain of the interview
with Mrs. Burman, supervening on her
alienation from Nesta, proves too much for
Nataly. She dies, the next evening, of heart-
disease, while Victor is at his first meeting.
He returns to find her gone, and the shock
drives him mad. By the irony of fate, the
news of Mrs. Burman's death arrives just at
this moment; she had died five and a half
hours after her younger rival.

Nesta† refuses Sowerby's renewed offer of
his hand; she marries Dartrey Fenellan whom
she owns "for leader, her fellow soldier,
warrior friend, hero, of her own heart's mould,
but a greater." Dartrey respected women,

---

* Like Beauchamp, he is under the domination of a single idea (see
below); but he only gets a tardy glimpse of the idea which Beauchamp
urged from the first, that the true aristocracy of the country must give a
lead to the people by showing them the right use of money, among other
things, and by abjuring the pursuit of luxury and self-display. Victor only
perceives this vaguely, and only after he has been chastened by a touch of
failure or a threatening of danger in his wild schemes (see chap. i).

† She recruits her health, like Harry Richmond, among the Alps.

instead of sentimentalising over them, and
this decides her in his favour.

The title of the story (taken from an earlier
tale) is semi-satirical. Victor Montgomery
Radnor does not prove a real victor in his
struggle against the world. He loses his cause,
his wife, and his reason. He is a successful
merchant, who regards money as a means to
higher things ; he is a man not of the world
but of ideas, generous, philanthropic, hospit-
able, intelligent, and chivalrous in his own
way ; he is faithful in all his relationships,
fond of music, and a brilliant host. But he is
conquered in the end, and the reason of his
defeat lies chiefly in his false attitude to life.
His demand for recognition at the hands of
conventional society is analysed as a violation
of Nature. "We are distracted, perverted,
made strangers to ourselves, by a false
position." In this subtle study of the incorrigible optimist, Meredith shows how Victor
suffers not only from the results of his initial
false step but from the fact that he allows his
wealth and social ambitions (equivalent to
circumstance or conventionality) to divert
him from his true self and turn him into an

object propelled by forces outside his control, which he cannot fathom. "He who has a scheme is the engine of it; he is no longer the man of his tastes or of his principles; . . . he is more the arrow to his bow than the bow to his arrow." Victor's enterprise thus acquires such a grasp of him as to precipitate him into courses of action, or rather of intrigues and scheming, which wreck the happiness of his wife and destroy his better self. He cannot bear to be beaten in his campaign against society. His fall on London Bridge is a dramatic reminder of the risks he is running; life had become the crossing of a bridge, with a slippery bit on it; but he waves off the reminder with the heat of wine and self-confidence. His spirit is unteachable, and the vanity of the man, nourished on his past series of successes, lures him on until he falls into the pit digged for him by his own folly.* In his power of deceiving himself and others for the time being he resembles Roy Richmond. Like him he cannot see the true

* Victor, like more than one of Meredith's leading characters, illustrates the Aristotelian maxim that the proper character for a tragedy is a prosperous, reputable man, who is wrecked not by vice or depravity but by some error.

strength and happiness of a simple life, or
the fact that the only success worth seeking
implies brotherhood and service of one
another, not any social triumph.

Victor's overpowering fascination and
magnetic personality lead him to treat Nataly
as a pleasant slave rather than as a true mate
—the common fault of those who fail in the
Meredith-romances.   The analysis of her
nature, with its loyalty to love, its heroic
devotion, its torture and perversion, is
masterly.   Victor declines to consult with his
wife; he prefers to plan for her on his own
account; and the result is that her wisdom
and better intuitions prove of no use to him.
It is only towards the end that Nataly, like
Vittoria, realises she would have done better
to resist her husband's glamour than to give in
to him as she has done.   She blames herself for
not having been stronger, and she plucks up
courage to act upon her own initiative; but it
is too late.   The main mischief has been done.
For this Meredith blames not the woman so
much as the conventional standards of society
which put her "into her woman's harness of
the bit and the blinkers, and taught to know

herself for the weak thing, the gentle parasite.
. . . And she must have a sufficient intelligence ; for her stupidity does not flatter the
possessing man. It is not an organic growth
that he desires in his mate, but a happy
composition." Nesta, the daughter, inherits
from her mother this hard-won lesson of
experience. She has "a nature pure and
sparkling as mid-sea foam," as her husband
once said of her; she reminds one of the
American girl at her best ; but she is a trifle
sententious, and it is Nataly who is the
heroine of the story. Victor's bright spirits had
been at first her rescue from a morbid despair ;
"he raised the head of the young flower from
its contemplation of grave-mould." But, by
the irony of events, it was his irrepressible
optimism which crushed this lily among
women. One of Meredith's loveliest stanzas
describes a bright morning after a stormy night:
    "As beholds her flowers
    Earth, from a night of frosty wreck,
    Enrobed in morning's mounted fire,
    When lowly, with a broken neck,
    The crocus lays her cheek to mire."
We cannot but think of that stanza when we

George Meredith

read poor Nataly's fate. All her instincts were for the normal civilisation, and circumstances made her a rebel! She never regretted her push for love, but she was obliged, by her husband's uncontrolled ambition, to take part in a struggle for recognition at the hands of a world whose laws they had, in all good conscience, broken. Her flower-like nature collapses under the illogical strain.* The pathos and tragedy of her lot form one of Meredith's great successes in psychological analysis and creative art.

As for minor points: note the glimpses of London (e.g. in ch. v: "and if haply down an alley some olive mechanic of street-organs has quickened little children's legs to rhythmic footing, they strike on thoughts braver than pastoral") which often recall Henley's lines "In the Dials" and his "London Voluntaries"; "One of Our Conquerors" is more of a London book than even "Rhoda Fleming." Meredith's whole vision of the squalor and romance of London-life ("a thing for hospital operations rather than for poetic rhapsody")

---

* The crocus-simile is applied, less tragically, to Ottilia in the twenty-fourth chapter of "The Adventures of Harry Richmond."

in this chapter is a pendant to de Quincey's famous seventh chapter in his "Autobiographic Sketches." His appreciative attitude towards the Salvation Army in the person of Matilda Pridden answers to the poem on "Jump to Glory Jane" which had appeared two years before.

The sketch of Skepsey, the clerk with a love of boxing, has the breath of Dickens about it, but it is more than caricature. The insistence (in ch. v) upon the inadequacy of satire to fulfil the conditions of song, which is the test of sanity, was echoed next year in "The Empty Purse":—

"Ask of thyself: this furious Yea
　Of a speech I thump to repeat,
In the cause I would have prevail,
　For seed of a nourishing wheat,
　　Is it accepted of Song?
Does it sound to the mind through the ear,
　Right sober, pure sane? has it
　　disciplined feet?
Thou wilt find it a test severe ;
　Unerring whatever the theme."

There are more farthings among the gold pieces in this novel than in almost any of its

329

predecessors, but now and then we get a sterling thought, tersely or daintily stamped, e.g., "If you would like a further definition of genius, think of it as a form of swiftness." "Look upon bouquets and clusters, and the idea of woman springs up at once." "Modern Realists imagine it's an exposition of positive human nature, when they've pulled down our noses to the worst parts." "The very meaning of having a heart, is to suffer through others or for them." "One of the scraps of practical wisdom gained by hardened sufferers is to keep from spying at horizons when they drop into a pleasant dingle." Note also the analysis of the French character in ch. x, the epigram on clubs (ch. xiii), and the witty sketch of Mr. Inchling in ch. xviii.

The wine-chapters (iii—iv) are a fresh reminder that Meredith's leading characters are apt to be what Rabelais called *beuverge*, i.e. addicted and inclined to wine ; but Meredith does not go to the length of Peacock*

* In "Fraser's Magazine" for October, 1857, Peacock wrote an essay on "The Bacchic Birth of Poetry," in order to prove that good poetry depended on good liquor, and the same vinous enthusiasm reappears in the second chapter of "The Misfortunes of Elphin." The sentence in the preface to a re-issue of his novels (1837), that "the fastidious in old wine are a race that does not decay," has quite a Meredithian flavour about it.

in his glorification of conviviality, and in
this novel he expressly adds the aphorism:
"The fighter for conquering is the one
who can last and has the open brain; and
there you have a point against alcohol." His
enthusiasm for wine arises partly from his
desire to appreciate the full joys of the natural
life and also from his sense of its social effects.
Meredith's drinkers are not sots. Their very
taste in wine forms part of their culture.

Meredith does equal justice to the qualities
of the third source of happiness as defined in
"Wein, Weib, und Gesang." Next to the
Emilia novels, this is his most musical.
"What glory is it to a Gentleman," says
Richardson, "if he were even a fine Per-
former, that he can strike a String, touch a
Key, or sing a Song with the Grace and
Command of a hired Musician?" Meredith
takes a much more sympathetic and intelligent
view of music in relation to the upper classes.
Music drew Victor and Nataly together, and
it proved one of their consolations, but it was
music of a first-class order. They were not
pottering amateurs. Dudley Sowerby, indeed, when he played on the flute, "went

George Meredith

through the music somewhat like an inquisi-
tive tourist in a foreign town, conscientious
to get to the end of the work of pleasure."
But the rest are genuine musicians, and in
this they resemble several of Meredith's
larger figures. Beauchamp is unmusical, but
Redworth enjoys the opera intelligently and
sings himself; so does Diana. Meredith
acknowledges in "Sandra Belloni," as here,
the high genius of Beethoven, but in "One
of Our Conquerors" (see ch. xiii) he shows
his old preference for the earlier Italian opera
of melody as compared to Wagner. Vittoria
sings to the conspirators "a song of flourishes;
one of those beflowered arias in which the
notes flicker and leap like young flames."
Diana's favourite opera is the "Puritani,"
and Victor is fond of Corelli, "the old barley-
sugar of Bellini or a Donizetti-Serenade.
Never mind Wagner's tap of his pedagogue's
bâton—a cadence catches one still."

The allusions to a dramatic satire called
"The Rajah in London" are passable, though
Peacock's "Aristophanes in London," which
may have been its partial prototype, was
more vital to "Gryll Grange." But the

332

semi-allegorical tale of Delphica, which Colney
Durance is allowed to inflict upon his friends,
is simply intolerable. Dudley Sowerby
protested that it was neither fact nor fun, and
probably it was only the feeling that he was
talking to a lady—and to a friend of the
author—which prevented him from doing the
same justice to the subject as Alceste did to
the far-fetched lines of Oronte's sonnet.

LORD ORMONT
AND HIS AMINTA

Lord Ormont and His Aminta

THIS novel, published in book-form in 1894, is shorter and easier to read than either "One of Our Conquerors" or "The Amazing Marriage," but, although the style and the plot are simpler, it deals with much the same problem, viz. the false position created by (a) a marriage into which the man and woman have entered from motives other than genuine love, and (b) by the man's false pride afterwards. The basis of the story is the career of Charles Mordaunt, Earl of Peterborough, a brilliant and hot-headed soldier who served with distinction, especially in the Spanish war, but fell into disgrace with the authorities for his arbitrary actions in the field. Not until a few years before his death did he acknowledge that he had married Anastasia Robinson, a well-known vocalist, about a dozen years earlier. The historical germ of the novel was truer than in the case of "Diana of the Crossways," but the real interest of the book—which is more of a sketch than a finished picture—lies in the deft studies of character and in the analysis of the marriage-problem with which Meredith has enriched his pages.

The following is an analysis of the plot.

Lord Ormont is a major-general of cavalry, who had learnt riding before he was ten, fighting before he was twelve, and outpost duty in the Austrian frontier cavalry before he was twenty. He had served in the Peninsula, in Canada, and in India where his exploits as a cavalry leader and as a swordsman had won him high repute throughout the army. He is a courteous, gallant, and honourable soldier, with a lurid kind of reputation in the field of love, where he had been obliged to fight more than one duel.

An enthusiastic hero-worship * of Lord Ormont unites the boys and girls in two adjacent English schools. The former are headed by Matthew Weyburn, or Matey, whose father, Colonel Sidney Weyburn, had

---

* This is one of the traits common to Weyburn and Beauchamp. Another is that both were the sons of British officers.

Lord Ormont and His Aminta

died in a cavalry charge at Toulouse. The
girls are led by Aminta Farrell, or Browny, a
pretty brunette. Her face seems " a frontis-
piece of a romantic story some day to be read,"
and the romantic story begins before very long.
A flirtation between Matey and Browny ends
in the withdrawal of the latter from school to
live with her aunt near Dover. Matey also
leaves school soon afterwards. Unable to
enter the army for lack of money, he prepares
himself, by study abroad, for a schoolmaster's
career ; his idea being to form a cosmopolitan
school in the Bernese Alps, where boys and
girls of any nationality or religion can be
trained together, and Old England taught to the
Continent, as the Continent to Old England.

Meantime, a daring exploit of Lord Ormont
brings him into conflict with the political
authorities in India, and he continues the
controversy by writing letters to the English
newspapers. Disgusted at the way he has
been treated, he returns home to nurse his
resentment of the country's black ingratitude.
A year or two later, when travelling in Spain
he meets Aminta and her aunt. Aminta has
Spanish blood in her, and she retains her

girlish worship for Lord Ormont, the hero of her schooldays. They are married at Madrid; he actuated by admiration for Aminta's style and beauty, and also by an impulse of satisfaction with her obvious hero-worship, which falls like balm upon his wounded pride; she, not in love so much as in the sentimental passion of a girl not yet out of her teens for a man whom she has idealised. The romance does not last very long. Aminta soon discovers that it is one thing to worship a hero, another thing to marry him. Lord Ormont, soured and angry at his country for having broken his military career and ridiculed his part in the newspaper controversy, refuses curtly to return to England with his bride; when eventually he does so, after seven years, he declines to enter English society. He prefers to sulk in his tent. He regards Aminta's natural desire for social recognition as erratic and disloyal, and he fails to see that this inaction on his part is a covert reflection on his wife. His relatives, especially Lady Charlotte Eglett, his sister, knowing his reputation and character, decline to believe that he has married the girl; the result is that she appears to society in the rôle of a Lady Doubtful, and this false position, in which his wounded pride has placed her, exposes Aminta to unpleasant gossip as well as to dangerous sympathy. Lord Ormont is too self-centred to realise this. He wishes to hit the world for having slighted him, and in doing so he hits the honour and happiness of his own wife. "A finer weapon," he reflects, "wherewith to strike at a churlish world was never given into the hands of man. These English may see in her, if they like, that they and their laws and customs are defied. It does her no hurt, and it hits them a ringing buffet." As a matter of fact, it does hurt Aminta. Her pride is wounded irreparably. She begins to criticise her hero, recognising his military and personal virtues but also his ignorance of the proper way to treat a woman and his disbelief "in her having equal life with him on earth." She has courage and nerve and capacity. But he neglects her claims to the status of a recognised wife, and insists on regarding her as a sort of puppet instead of as a comrade. The fact is, Lord Ormont's idea of managing a wife was practically that of managing a regiment ; his orders must be followed ; he gives the lead, "their's not to reason why, their's not to make reply."

Matters are brought to a head by the unintentional intervention of Matthew Weyburn, who is sent by Lady Eglett ostensibly to be private secretary to Lord Ormont and to assist him in the writing of his memoirs.* Lady Eglett's secondary motive for this action is bad. She thinks Weyburn's handsome figure may detach Aminta from Lord Ormont and so relieve the latter of an incubus. This dim hope is justified in a very different manner from what she expects. Matey and Browny eventually recognise each other, and their relationship becomes both delicate and equivocal. The old romantic passion stirs in them, though at first they are hardly conscious of it. But—as Meredith implies, in a subtle, almost hyper-subtle, analysis of their relations—they are too honourable to admit it even to themselves, though

---

* The allusion to the fit of panic over a threatened invasion (ch. ix) recalls the more detailed and equally sarcastic description in the first chapter of " Beauchamp's Career," and the lines " To Colonel Charles."

Lord Ormont and His Aminta

Aminta's admiration for Weyburn is as undisguised as his sympathy with her toneless, unhappy position in London and his contempt for Lord Ormont's perverse and cruel conduct. The latter adds to his offences by refusing to take his wife to Steignton, his country estate —a refusal which is naturally set down by Lady Eglett to the fact that her brother is heartily ashamed of his connexion with the girl. Lord Ormont then leaves for a visit to Paris, and in his absence the end of the business begins. Three incidents help to precipitate the crisis. One is the death of Weyburn's mother ; Aminta happens to be present, and the emotional strain * brings the pair of them closer together. Pity for her clouded position did not create his love for her, but it quickened it into a perilous warmth. The undesirable attentions of a London roué, Mr. Morsfield, further help to awaken Aminta to the slumbering capacities of passion in her nature, at the very moment when she realises that her affinity is Weyburn. Finally, she determines to pay a flying visit to

* With the passage on prayer (ch. xiv), compare Dr. Shrapnel's remarks. in "Beauchamp's Career" (ch. xxix).

George Meredith

Steignton on her own account, that she may
see the place where she might have been
happy. This impulse marks the ebb, not the
flow, of her belief in Lord Ormont. It is due
to the sense that he had now forfeited her
affection. The visit, she feels, will "close a
volume. She could not say why the volume
must be closed." As a matter of fact, she had
forgiven her husband, but, like Carinthia in
"The Amazing Marriage," "the shattering of
their union was the cost of forgiveness."
She is conscious that he has degraded her by
wounding her self-respect, " and what is a
woman's pride but the staff and banner of her
soul, beyond all gifts? He who wounds it
cannot be forgiven—never!—he has killed
the best of her." Meantime Lord Ormont
has partially relented. On hearing that his
wife had been refused presentation at Court,
he hurries home in order to prepare Steignton
for her reception and surprise her by thus
yielding to her wishes. He will bend his
pride thus far. She must give up all thoughts
of a London career, but, if she agrees to this,
he is willing to live with her at Steignton, and
so make amends to her for the past. "To

time and a wife it is no disgrace for a man to
bend. It is the form of submission of the
bulrush to the wind, of courtesy in the cavalier
to a lady." Lady Eglett, who has heard of
her brother's preparations at Steignton, drives
down with Weyburn to ascertain the reason
of it. They meet there Aminta and her aunt,
who had been joined on the road by Mr.
Morsfield, against Aminta's wishes. Lord
Ormont, in a fit of irritation, sends Aminta
back in charge of Weyburn, and, under the
tension of the moment, the two realise that
only honour keeps them from trembling into
one another's arms. Weyburn's self-command
prevails, however. He will not take advantage of the situation. Lord Ormont, too proud
to apologise to Aminta or to acknowledge that
he has wronged her, then tries to make some
practical amends in another direction by
taking a house for her on the Thames. But
Aminta's eyes are at last opened to his real
character and to the state of her own heart ;
the disillusionment is complete. After a
stubborn struggle, he induces his sister to part
with the family jewels, hoping by the gift of
them to propitiate Aminta, while at the same

George Meredith

time he arranges to fight a duel with Mr. Morsfield. But his repentance, like that of Lord Fleetwood in "The Amazing Marriage," comes too late.* Weyburn goes to say good-bye to her before leaving for Switzerland, and she realises that she must make a leap in the dark ; at any cost she must be clear of her husband : she returns the jewels to Lord Ormont, takes farewell of him by letter, and leaves his house to stay with her friends the Colletts. Weyburn meets her there by a sheer chance ; the two are surprised into a confession of their mutual love, and they resolve to elope to Switzerland. "We commit this indiscretion," Weyburn tells her frankly, "with a world against us, our love and labour are constantly on trial ; we must have great hearts, and if the world is hostile we are not to blame it. My own soul, we have to see that we do—though not publicly, not insolently, offend good citizenship. But we believe—I with my whole faith, and I may say it of you—that we are not offending Divine law." They start the school near

* "He said of his country: That Lout comes to a knowledge of his wants too late. But what if his words were flung at him in turn ? Short of 'Lout,' it rang correctly " (ch. xxx).

Lord Ormont and His Aminta

Berne. Seven years later, Lord Ormont, who
chances to visit it, places his grand-nephew
there; he retains no rancour in his heart
against Weyburn, and he magnanimously
believes in the purity and justice of Aminta.
Six months later, his death makes it possible
for the pair to marry one another.

The novel, like more than one of Meredith's
stories, serves to illustrate the remark of
Payne Knight, which Peacock applied to
Shelley's marriage, that "the same kind of
marriage which usually ends a comedy as
usually begins a tragedy." Only, Aminta and
Weyburn end in bliss. The justification of their
offence against the conventions of the world
is found in the power, conferred on them by
their union, "to make amends to the world."
They realise that they do not "go together
into a garden of roses." They unite their
lives because each can be a true mate to the
other in the career of service* opening before

* Meredith, in ch. v, comments on "the hardest of the schoolmaster's
tasks—away fly the boys in sheaves. After his toil with them, to instruct,
restrain, animate, their minds, they leave him, they plunge into the world
and are gone. To sustain his belief that he has done serviceable work, he
must be sure of his having charged them with good matter." This faith
and faithfulness in sowing is, of course, the dominant thought in poems
like "Seed-Time" and "The Question Whither."

347

George Meredith

them, whereas Lord Ormont had denied Aminta any comradeship or rights in the married state, till her mind was repressed and her spirits deadened. The tragic injustice of the marriage was checked, Meredith argues, by the courage of Aminta and her lover. "Hardly blushing, she walks on into the new life beside him, and hears him say: 'I in my way, you in yours; we are equals, the stronger for being equals,' and she quite agrees, and she gives him the fuller heart for his not requiring her to be absorbed—she is the braver mate for him." This description of Meredith's ideal for a wife, which occurs in the sixteenth chapter, tallies with his other definitions in "Diana" (ch. xiv) and "The Tragic Comedians" (ch. vii) as well as elsewhere.

Meredith usually prefers to take an only child or son as his central figure, but here, as in "The Amazing Marriage" (and to a lesser degree in "Evan Harrington" or in "Beauchamp's Career," where Renée and her brother are secondary figures), he delineates brother and sister.* Lord Ormont and his

* Compare the passage on the love of brother and sister in ch. xxi with George Eliot's poem " Brother and Sister."

sister are quite the most vital characters in the story. Lady Charlotte Eglett is one of Meredith's cleverest studies in the middle-aged aristocratic lady; she has a stinging tongue, intense family affection, Tory prejudices, and a keen brain. Like Lady Jocelyn, in "Evan Harrington," she loves to read Memoirs, and she is much stronger than her husband. "They were excellent friends. Few couples can say more." The foil to her is Mrs. Nargett Pagnell, the vulgar, scheming widow of a solicitor, who has the social ambition of a feminine snob and "a tongue," as Lady Charlotte remarked, "that goes like the reel of a rod, with a pike bolting out of the shallows to the snag he knows — to wind round it and defy you to pull." She engages in a game of Pull with Lord Ormont, using his wife as a lever, and repeatedly exasperating the husband by her offensive intrigues. Her influence on him resembles that exerted by Harriet's sister upon Shelley; it involves the innocent wife in the repugnance of the husband for her relatives. At the same time, it must be allowed that Aminta's toleration of her aunt is a weak point in the story, or at least in her character.

Pride is more conspicuous than sentiment- alism in the plot. Aminta's error lay partially in her undisciplined and sentimen- tal passion for this modern Coriolanus, but in her and in her husband the right and the wrong sort of pride are dominant.* Pride, in its particular form of underbred social ambition, is represented by Mrs. Pagnell, who makes nearly the same kind of mischief by her attempt to excite Lord Ormont's jealousy and force his hand as the Countess de Saldar in "Evan Har- rington."

Besides several bits of impressionism, aptly thrown in, there are three capital passages of descriptive narrative : the ride behind a postillion back from Steignton (ch. xviii—xx), which recalls the well-known ride in "Diana of the Crossways" (ch. xi) ; the

---

* In ch. ix the English capacity for taking a licking well is praised, as in "The Egoist" (ch- ix) ; the same chapter contains Weyburn's criticism of Lord Ormont's sore temper as "a curmudgeonly, humping solitariness, that won't forgive an injury, nurses rancour, smacks itself in the face, because it can't—to use the old schoolboy words—take a licking!"

Lord Ormont and His Aminta

day on the Thames * (ch. xxiv); and the
swimming-scene or marine duet in ch. xxvii.
The school-scenes † are not inferior to those
in "The Adventures of Harry Richmond,"
though their scale is smaller, but nothing in
that novel surpasses the incisive analysis,
given by Weyburn to Lady Eglett, of "men
of brains" and "men of aptitude" (ch. xiii)—
a caustic and penetrating piece of psychological discernment. Among the minor
characters, the Anglican clergyman gets the
same hard knocks as his fellows in "The
Adventures of Harry Richmond" and "One

* A poetical sketch of this scenery was drawn in one of the pastorals in
the first volume of his poems. Compare especially these hexameters, which
Kingsley singled out for praise :—

"O joy thus to revel all day in the grass of our own beloved country;
    Revel all day till the lark mounts at eve with his sweet 'tirra-lirra,'
    Thrilling delightfully. See on the river the slow rippled surface
    Shining; the slow ripple broadens in circles; the bright surface
        smoothens. . . .
    There by the wet-mirror'd osiers, the emerald wing of the kingfisher
    Flashes, the fish in his beak! There the dabchick dived, and the motion
    Lazily undulates all thro' the tall standing army of rushes.
    O joy thus to revel all day, till the twilight turns us homeward!
    Till all the lingering, deep-blooming splendour of sunset is over,
    And the one star shines mildly in mellowing hues, like a spirit
    Sent to assure us that light never dieth, tho' day is now buried."

† Boys, however, do not feel as they are said to feel about Browny in
ch. i. The description is as Meredithian as that of the sailor's feelings in
ch. xxvi, which also contains one of the few lapses into Meredi hese
throughout the entire novel—"the unwonted supper in them withheld an
answer to the intimidating knock." The purport of this cryptic utterance
is that a heavy supper made them sleep soundly in the morning.

George Meredith

of Our Conquerors," while Mrs. Lawrence
Finchley and the circle of London pleasure-
lovers are painted in the same colours as their
predecessors in "The Ordeal of Richard
Feverel."

Lady Eglett's brief appreciation of the
Jewish character, in ch. xvi, is a foil to the
less sympathetic references in "The Tragic
Comedians" and "One of Our Conquerors."
The eulogy on boxing (in ch. iii) tallies with
the similar allusions in "Rhoda Fleming,"
"One of Our Conquerors," and "The
Amazing Marriage."

THE AMAZING MARRIAGE

w

The Amazing Marriage

THIS rich and striking novel, the last which came from Meredith's pen, appeared in 1895, about the same time as "Jude the Obscure," and wits of the day suggested that the proper titles would be "The Obscure Marriage" and "The Amazing Jude." The criticism was more clever than just. There is little or no obscurity about the motives and results of the marriage between Carinthia and Lord Fleetwood, although there is a good deal to amaze the reader. The book forms a curious contrast to "Lord Ormont and his Aminta." In both stories the heroine's character is developed through ill-treatment at her husband's hands; but instead of driving her to vice or, as in the case of Aminta, to elope with a worthy lover, the discipline of injustice matures the heroine of this story within her legal position. She refuses to live with her husband, but she will not take

355

another man. Both Carinthia and Aminta
are flung on the world ; both, on Meredith's
reading of their lives, are of equal purity, but
they differ in their growth.

The book is an account of the amazing
prelude and the more amazing outcome of
the marriage between Lord Fleetwood and
Carinthia Jane Kirby. The main facts of the
story are as follows.

When close upon his seventieth year,
Captain John Peter Avason Kirby, who came
of old Lincolnshire stock "and claimed
descent from a chief of the Danish rovers,"
ran off openly and skilfully with the Countess
of Cressett, a lovely and spirited Irish girl
aged twenty-three. She had been wooed
rapidly by her husband, who excelled as a
four-in-hand coachman. But as "she could
not always be on the top of a coach, which
was his throne of happiness," the young couple
fell apart after a year of matrimony. Meanwhile Captain Kirby, "the old Buccaneer,"
"with his great white beard and hair—not a
lock of it shed—and his bronze lion-face,"
captivated the heart of the Countess, and was
in turn captivated by her. Friendship passed

The Amazing Marriage

into infatuation, and at midnight on the 21st of June, the sturdy sailor outwitted the London cavaliers of the Countess Fanny (so-called from a popular ballad on the subject), who eloped with her hero to the Continent. Lord Cressett took his wife's flight philosophically. "Ah! Fan!" was all he said, "she never would run in my ribbons." He declined to pursue the pair, and died a fortnight later, having fallen from his coach-box in a fit. Thereupon the Captain and his Countess were married in Switzerland, where their first child was born eleven months afterwards; he was christened Chillon Switzer John Kirby after his birthplace and his father. The Captain then settled in Carinthia, on the borders of Styria, where he purchased and worked a mine; there his second child, the heroine of this story, was born, and christened* Carinthia Jane.

* "All novelists," Scott declares in the preface to 'Ivanhoe,' "have had occasion at some time or other to wish with Falstaff that they knew where a commodity of good names was to be had." Meredith was particularly rich and happy in this department. The geographical names of the Kirbys are perhaps among his least successful efforts, but the nomenclature of the novel does not show any dearth of inventiveness or lapse into unreality otherwise.

George Meredith

After being educated in England and serving a term in the German army, the son was sent back to adopt a military career in England, where he devoted himself to explosive inventions together with his uncle Lord Levellier. The separation together with the fear of English scandal quenching her son's love killed his mother before long, and a week later her loyal disconsolate husband followed her. When the action of the story proper begins, the brother and sister, aged twenty-three and twenty-one respectively, are leaving their old home in the mountains for England, where Chillon had determined that Carinthia should live under the guardianship of their uncle, a miserly nobleman, at Lekkatts (popularly known as "Leancats"). She is described as a girl of red-gold hair, rugged brows, fine physique and fair education.

Their immediate destination is Baden, where Chillon hopes to meet his lady-love, Miss Henrietta Fakenham, only daughter of Commodore Baldwin Fakenham, whose elder brother Curtis had been an unsuccessful rival of Captain Kirby in wooing the Countess of Cressett. Henrietta is travelling with her

The Amazing Marriage

ather and her cousin Livia. The latter, a
daughter of Curtis, was "the young widow of
Lord Duffield when she accepted the Earl of
Fleetwood, and was his third countess, and
again a widow at eight-and-twenty." The Earl
of Fleetwood's great wealth, due to a previous
marriage (engineered by Captain Kirby) with
a Welsh heiress, had passed to Livia's step-son
Russell, the Earl of Fleetwood, who is the
hero of the story. His money and generosity
enable his beautiful young step-mother to
gratify a passion for gambling, which she
indulges by means of her attendant cavaliers.
In return for this, as well as with a view
to retaining her hold of the capricious, self-
willed Earl, she schemes to further his suit to
Henrietta, in pursuit of whom the young
nobleman is now travelling on the Continent.

Walking over the mountains, Chillon and
his sister overtake and render some aid to a
young English tourist, Gower Woodseer, an
impressionable lover of Nature and phrases,
with a Bohemian philosophy curiously
opposed to the Dissenting faith of his Welsh
father, a shoemaker and preacher in Whitechapel. Woodseer's heart is divided between

a passion for mountains and a thirst for style, and when he and Lord Fleetwood happen to meet some days later, they strike up a young man's friendship, which ends in the enthusiastic young nobleman carrying off his plebeian comrade for a week's walking-tour.* Their admiration of the picturesque and mountainous in Nature is varied by discussions of Carinthia whom (without knowing more than her name) Woodseer had described in his note-book as "a beautiful Gorgon—a haggard Venus." The phrase arrests Lord Fleetwood's fancy, and, with a sentimental interest in the fair unknown, he pictures her face thus hinted. It haunts him. Even the phrase "Carinthia Saint and Martyr" catches the very man who, by the irony of events, is to be the agent of her martyrdom. From Woodseer's hint of description and further talk, he conjures up the vision of this woman. "That's a face high over beauty. Just to know there is a woman like her, is an antidote." Lord Fleetwood prides himself on his know-

---

* This passion for walking was characteristic of Meredith himself. He would have subscribed with heartiness, in all likelihood, to the spirit of Nietzsche's saying that "sedentary application is the sin against the Holy Ghost. Only thoughts won by walking are valuable."

The Amazing Marriage

ledge of women, and at once rushes off to idealise this rock-like heroine of his friend's diary. "Tell me you met her, you saw her. I want only to hear she lives, she is in the world." Woodseer fails to ascribe this sentimental craving to its true source, or to diagnose the youthful malady of "one bitten by the serpent of love, and athirst for an image of the sex to serve for the cooling herb." A casual remark of the Earl seems to show that he is already jealous of Henrietta and (perhaps) Chillon—"Beautiful women compared to roses may whirl away with their handsome dragoons! A pang from them is a thing to be ashamed of! And there are men who trot about, whining with it!" Anyhow, the second-hand vision of Carinthia comes at an apt psychological moment in the young inflammable lord's development, although he is rather damped to find from Woodseer that she is a woman, not a mere girl, for, like Sir Willoughby Patterne, he would sentimentally exclude the world, and "woman" suggests that intrusive object.

The two strangely yoked comrades finally join Lord Fleetwood's party at Baden, where

George Meredith

Woodseer falls under the spell of Livia, dips into what his father terms the "spotty business" of gaming, and has to tramp home penniless to London.

Meanwhile, Henrietta had accompanied her father to cavalry manœuvres near Carlsruhe. There Chillon and Carinthia find her, and the former leaves for England, whilst the rest rejoin the Countess Livia at Baden, where Lord Fleetwood had promised Henrietta to attend a ball at the ducal Schloss. Unfortunately he hears of Henrietta having escorted Chillon part of the road on his departure and having returned with red eyes from the farewell. This news adds fuel to the Earl's displeasure at Miss Fakenham. Wounded by her coquettish behaviour, and resenting the poison of her fascination, he proudly withdraws from the sight of her to spend the night at a neigbouring village. The next morning he accidentally comes upon Carinthia (without knowing who she is) stepping gracefully, daringly, and nimbly along a horizontal pine-stem jutting out from a mountain-precipice. Ever at her best among the mountains, "where the cold engraving of her face became a picture of colour," the girl appealed instantly to Lord Fleetwood's sense of the picturesque as "a noble daughter of the woods. Not comparable to Henrietta in feminine beauty, she was on an upper plateau," with "a savage poignancy in serenity" stamped on her face, intrepid, individual, full of character. She seemed to him akin to the sort of Carinthia which Woodseer had described; and, as he spent the day alone among the woods, "the course of the poison Henrietta infused, and to which it disgraced him to be so subject," was more than diverted by the inner contemplation of this girl. A single glimpse of her "raised him out of his grovelling perturbations, cooled and strengthened him."

Still, when night came, to the ball he had to go. He was the prisoner of his word, or it suited his humour to think so. One key to his character and conduct is repeatedly described by Meredith as a proud ambition never to go back from a promise. It is the comic element in his nature, and from it the tragedy oozes. The rarest of gentlemen on this point of honour, and punctilious to

George Meredith

chivalry, he considered himself bound by his lightest word, no matter what were the consequences. "His pride," as Henrietta said once, "is in his word, and supposing he's in love, it's with his pride, which never quits him." Down he goes therefore to fulfil this distasteful engagement by looking in for a few moments at the Schloss. *Dis aliter uisum.* At the castle he meets Woodseer's Carinthia, the girl he had seen that morning in the woods, but now brilliant in the glow and glamour of her first ball. During their third dance he pleads imperiously for her to marry him, and is accepted.

This, the first amazing step in the story of an amazing marriage, seems at first sight abrupt and improbable. Meredith, as usual, narrates the incident indirectly, putting the whole account of the ball into a letter (ch. xii) from Henrietta to Chillon. But he has not failed to suggest motives on both sides for the step, and these become visible, if not very credible, on a careful perusal of the novel.

On neither side is love the primary motive. Carinthia's love of her brother and desire to relieve him of the burden of supporting her had already turned her unselfish innocent thoughts to matrimony as one means by which she might further his prospects and enable him to marry Henrietta. On their last walk, she had asked in distress how she could avoid burdening him, and he had lightly replied, "Marry, and be a blessing to a husband." The words whispered to her also of a possible escape from her avaricious uncle's guardianship. But, conscious of her inadequate physical attractions and of her lack of fortune, she feels she would be humbly grateful to "the noble, knightly gentleman who would really stoop to take a plain girl by the hand." To this sentimental feeling must be added her scanty previous knowledge of Lord Fleetwood as a lover of the mountains and a rival of her brother in Henrietta's love. Before ever the two met, the woman had dreamt of some lordly, attractive, irresistible youth, who should claim rather than supplicate a woman's stricken heart. Flushed by such aims and expectations, romantic or otherwise, Carinthia was obviously tinder to the spark flung down by the young earl's impetuous wooing. She

365

yielded to him, gravely, irrevocably, and with all her soul.

Upon his side the motives appear to have been more complex; they were so elusive that they characterise his action as a sudden freak. His restless eyes indicated an ill-regulated spirit, capable of sudden shifts under any stress of passion. He had come to the ball smarting under a sense of injury at Henrietta's coquetry, which humiliated his pride. He found there the fair unknown, whom he had ardently discussed with Woodseer and subsequently seen with his own admiring eyes. He saw her, too, in a fresh and brilliant aspect, irradiated with "the something above beauty"—to quote Henrietta's letter—"more unique and impressive—like the Alpine snow-cloak towering up from the flowery slopes." Thus the rebound of wounded jealous pride was caught upon the vision of this brilliant, stedfast creature, who satisfied "his passion for the wondrous in the look of a woman's face" and was innocent of shifty dealings with mankind. The mad impulse of his proposal was consonant with the erratic, splendid character of an aristocratic dragon-fly, who had inherited Celtic sentimentality as well as a strain of eccentricity from his mother, and whilst the quixotic circumstances of his engagement roused astonishment and consternation in his own circle and beyond it, they were not wholly inexplicable to those who were familiar with his overbearing, impulsive disposition.

Amazement followed amazement. The next morning, Lord Fleetwood disappeared without a word to anyone. Reflection had brought him the intolerable sense of being now in bondage. "Prone to admire and bend the knee when he admired, he chafed at subjection, unless he had the particular spell constantly renewed." His pride resented any encroachment on its freedom, for that threatened to interfere with his ambition to lead others, and in a black fit of re-action he became desperate, even relentless and unscrupulous, in the attempt to get quit of this girl of poor birth who had—he perversely imagined—ensnared his word and captured him by some illusion of the senses. He made off for Wales, "supposing, as he well might, that his latest mad freak of the proposal of his hand and title to the strange girl in a quadrille at a foreign castle" would presently be forgotten by her, when nothing more was said about it. In the course of time all risk of annoyance on the subject would blow over.

Carinthia, however, was built otherwise; as we know, she was prepared to look upon her engagement with very different eyes. Lord Fleetwood's disappearance and silence were accepted by her quietly as part and parcel of the whole strange affair. Crossing to England, she stayed two months with Admiral Fakenham in Hampshire, "patiently expecting and rebuking the unmaidenliness of her expectations, as honest young women in her position used to do." Her humble gratitude for being chosen at all by a husband kept her still unsuspicious of any estrangement or foul play on his part.

Meanwhile, to protect her reputation and interests, or to save himself from the cost of maintaining her, Lord Levellier put himself into action. He surprised Lord Fleetwood, who had returned to London, imagining he had done penance for his impulsiveness and got rid of his fetters. A message was wrung

368

The Amazing Marriage

from him to the effect that although "not particularly fitted for the married state," he asked Carinthia whether it was her wish that he should marry her. The first warning clause of the communication never reached Carinthia. Her answer would have been the same, says Meredith, even had she heard it. But she did not get her odd lover's preliminary warning, perhaps because it was suppressed by the miserly Lord Levellier who was interested in getting his niece married to a wealthy husband, or because Chillon and Henrietta, by a sort of half-innocent intrigue, omitted to repeat it, in the hope that her marriage would promote, as it did promote, their own engagement and marriage. Chillon, at any rate, blamed himself afterwards for the curtailed version of the reluctant bridegroom's message. Neither he nor Henrietta, both of whom knew Lord Fleetwood's character, took the responsibility of standing out against the marriage. It suited their own scheme excellently when Carinthia replied simply and directly to the Earl's question, "Oh, I will, I am ready, tell him." The intriguing Livia persuades her to refrain from either writing or worrying him for a fulfilment of his promise. But piqued at the marriage of Chillon and Henrietta, he at last yields to the dunning demands of Lord Levellier by despatching the following insolent note written on the tenth of the month:—"My Lord: I drive to your church-door on the fourteenth of the month at ten a.m., to keep my appointment with Miss C. J. Kirby, if I do not blunder the initials. Your Lordship's obedient servant, Fleetwood." Lord Levellier transmits the peremptory summons, but not the letter, to Carinthia. Three days after she heard it, she was married to a man to whom she had not spoken since the night of their sudden engagement.

As Chillon was absent on his honeymoon, and Admiral Fakenham suddenly prostrated with a fierce attack of gout, no male relative of the bride was present to witness the amazing marriage, except Lord Levellier who was not anxious to see anything strange in a bridegroom appearing at the altar in coaching costume. For with delicate consideration Lord Fleetwood, who had a pugilist inside his carriage, put his wife on the box and drove her forthwith to witness a prize-fight, which

The Amazing Marriage

he had pledged himself to attend, between his protégé, Kit Ines, and another bruiser patronised by Lord Brailstone. The day resembled that on which Carinthia had first landed in England some months before ; it was wild, dark, threatening, and with this auspicious setting of weather and occupation, her married life began under a cloud of the noble earl's black spite and temper.

" Was ever woman in this fashion wooed ?
Was ever woman in this fashion won ? "

If the prelude to the marriage was amazing, its consequences are more amazing still. *En route* to the prize-fight, Lord Fleetwood behaves with the sullenness and insolence of an aristocrat who chooses to regard himself as cleverly entrapped into matrimony by a scheming girl and her relatives. The bad stuff in his character rises to the surface. Recollections of Baden mock him. Having lost Henrietta, he is doubly piqued to find himself bound for life to the sister of his successful rival, to a wife whose father came of no creditable stock. By the irony of fate, he is tied to her by his own word. "He was renowned and unrivalled as the man of stainless honour : the one living man of his word. There was his distinction among the herd. . . But, by all that is holy, he pays for his distinction." And dishonourably, even brutally, he is in the humour to make the girl pay too, by treating her with a studied cruelty of speech and silence which springs from his devilish enjoyment of the irony in their situation. His own idiocy, or what he chooses to regard as such, is visited upon Carinthia. She had completed her crimes by failing to appear at the altar in the same radiant splendour as on the night of the ball at Baden. And his lordship's aggrieved soul resents even her natural address, "My husband." It was "a manner of saying 'my fish'"! Meanwhile poor Carinthia sits beside him, hungry to admire and trust, for all her self-possession. Innocent of intrigue, she recalls him as he was at Baden, and feels herself "passionately grateful for humbleness exalted, virginly sensible of treasures of love to give." She had put her life into her husband's hands, and was content, but her trust is quickly and grimly repaid. After the prize-fight (described in Meredith's best manner), at which Kit Ines

The Amazing Marriage

vanquishes his opponent, my lord returns with
her to an inn where he heartlessly leaves her,
driving off to spend the evening at Canleys
with his own set. Had he not pledged his
word to attend this ball? A Whitechapel girl,
Madge Winch, who follows the fortunes of
Kit Ines, is left to attend Carinthia, who sits
stunned and suffering under such treatment
yet enduring it meekly. "Pain breathed out
of her, and not a sign of pain was visible."
The sympathy and admiration of Madge
were almost her only consolation on her
wedding-night.

Almost; for Lord Fleetwood was impressionable and had his moments of amorous
weakness. Driving back alone after midnight,
he climbed by a ladder to her window; when
she sprang from her bed to defend herself, he
saw "the look of steel melting into the bridal
flower," as she recognised her husband in the
intruder and received him with passionate joy.
Yet even this revelation of her charms failed
to move him from his pride or to appease the
black resentment that still tore him away from
her. "The devil in him" was " still insatiate
for revenge upon her who held him to his

word," and after this midnight hurried visit he disappeared. He tried to indemnify himself for the yoke of marriage by making his capturer smart still more. The day after his marriage he was in the House of Lords, "and then went down to his estates in Wales, being an excellent holder of the reins, whether on the coach-box or over the cash-box." While there, he ruminates on the advisability of following a suggestion of his weak young friend, Lord Feltre, a Roman Catholic peer whose recipe for the soul entangled by women is religion ; monasticism seems to offer a possible, honourable escape from life-long bondage to the "beautiful Gorgon." Woodseer had once said it was a question of the man or the monk with him, and that, unless he chose to treat women frankly as part of the Nature whom he pretended to love, instead of cynically viewing them as temptresses or victims of the male, he was on the straight road to a cowl. Lord Fleetwood, in his fresh dilemma, dallies with the latter course. But the mood is only a passing fit.

Meantime this mess of a marriage had had its effects upon Carinthia. She walked to the

The Amazing Marriage

Earl's Kentish seat, Esslemont, but failed to
find him. After staying on till her heart was
broken, she resolved to leave the inn, where
Lord Fleetwood had ordered all her expenses
to be paid, although he left her penniless.
Walking part of the way, she came to London
with her loyal humble friend, Madge Winch,
and lodged in Whitechapel with the latter's
sister in a greengrocer's shop. There she is
found by Gower Woodseer, whose father is
acquainted with the Winches. Gower is
is despatched to inform Admiral Fakenham,
whose gout alone prevents him from executing
his wrathful purpose of rising to champion his
injured favourite in London. A letter is
written by the Admiral to Lady Arpington,
whose mother had known Countess Fanny,
begging her to give temporary shelter to
Carinthia ; but this missive is wiled out of
Woodseer's hands by Livia. The Admiral's
death, however, sets the youth free, and he
informs Lady Arpington of all that has trans-
pired. She hotly summons the Earl, who is
a connection of her own. He has just returned
to London, "disposed for marital humaneness
and jog-trot harmony, by condescension."

George Meredith

Since his marriage, as he is forced to admit, his black devil had been partly exorcised. His memory of her charm at the midnight interview inclines him to think her love must be sincere. Impressed with these better feelings of tolerance and magnanimity, he goes to his interview with Lady Arpington, rather inclined to relent and take up his wife again, but in no sense ashamed or sorry for his past conduct. And it is this false pride which again thwarts his better purposes. For underneath these lay a desire to find "solace for the hurt to his pride in spreading a snare for the beautiful Henrietta," by using his money to work upon her love of luxury and music. If he succeeded with this butterfly of a Riette, it would appease his wrath at her for having refused him and also tied him to Carinthia; besides, her weak conduct would justify his lordship's contempt for her and show him what a fine fate he had escaped in an alliance with her. He was moved by jealousy and vindictiveness and selfishness, not love. All he wanted was to know she was purchasable, not to possess or taste her fascinations for himself again. The mere proof that she was accessible to seduction, would "release him from vile subjection to one of the female heap," and by this sacrifice or (at least) this crucial temptation of the coquette his lordship's blood would be washed clean of her image. By means of this "formless plot," with "a shade of the devilish in it, he acknowledged," he would be able to despise Henrietta and so to crush out the sparks which she had kindled in his inflammable soul, and which he angrily found himself unable otherwise to quench. Besides, it would be a blow struck at Chillon, his successful rival, and through him at Carinthia. The malice of the scheme was only a degree worse than that which had made him lure Woodseer to gamble at Baden.

This pleasant intrigue had fallen into abeyance during his temporary residence with Lord Feltre. But it is roused, and with it the eccentric aristocrat's dogged pride, by Lady Arpington's reproaches and report. His tender sensibilities are rudely irritated by the news of poor Carinthia's flight to White-chapel. The man becomes iron and ice at once. Entirely ignoring the position in which his own conduct had left her, he chooses to

George Meredith

resent her action as a personal insult, which he interprets as a clever stroke at himself; to his cynical theory of women, it seems "a move worthy the daughter of the old Buccaneer," crafty and deliberate. Consequently, he refuses all intercourse with her, and the epithet "Countess of Whitechapel," with which London gossip and ridicule decorated her, is set down by his wounded pride as a fresh dart of the enemy.* He sullenly remains in the West-End, occasionally visited by his good genius, Gower Woodseer. For he is his own Iago. Carinthia never gives him occasion to be jealous. She resists the entreaties of Chillon and Henrietta, and stays on in her Whitechapel obscurity, tending the poor. She will not accept the Earl's offer of his country-seat Esslemont. Her one desire and claim of love is to meet him. Hearing through Kit Ines that his lordship and party are to visit Vauxhall Gardens one evening in June, Madge takes her mistress there, and in the midst of a disturbance Carinthia commits the mortal offence of coming coolly to her

* His resentment reminds one of the French naturalist who described a certain animal as "trés méchant,—quand on l'attaque, il se défend."

The Amazing Marriage

husband's assistance with a stick. This is an
unpardonable outrage to his dignity ! He sees
this malignant woman pestering him with
unwelcome attentions, thwarting and goading
him perpetually, posing as "a demoiselle
Moll Flanders," and covering her liege lord
with derision and ridicule before the world.
He chooses to think that she is persecuting
him. Then, being a man of quick temper and
few scruples, he makes a wanton reprisal for
this imaginary insult by employing his prizefighter to kidnap Madge and Carinthia.
Thanks to the former and Gower Woodseer,
Carinthia escapes from her suburban villa
next morning. Accompanied by Gower, she
manages to reach her husband's town-house ;
but finding her there on his return from a
morning-ride, he withdraws haughtily to a
neighbouring hotel, still refusing a personal
interview to the lady who bore his title. His
"erratic, if not mad, and in any case ugly,
conduct" becomes now a mixture of fast
living and sentimental philandering with
Catholicism ; while Carinthia, who has
Henrietta to live with her and frequent
visits from Woodseer to enliven her, is

379

content to endure for a time this dog's treatment in what London merrily termed "the Battle of the Spouses."

The intolerable strain of her position is relieved by a journey to Wales, for which his lordship with scrupulous justice provides the money, though he still refuses her a shilling for her own purse. On the 11th of December, she gives birth to a son. The news of this reaches her husband on his return from a yachting cruise with Lord Feltre, but it is simply a grosser offence and irritation to his smarting dignity. Again the twisted workings of his pride urge him to carry on his plot against Henrietta. Besides, the absence of any communication from Carinthia herself is surely an added insult. "She sulked! after besmutting the name she had filched from him, she let him understand that there was no intention to repent. Possibly she meant war." At all events, "the crowd of his grievances with the woman rushed pell-mell, deluging young shoots of sweeter feelings" in his petulant, egotistic soul. Yet one symptom of sanity appears in his generosity to Sarah Winch, Madge's

The Amazing Marriage

sister, whom—out of gratitude for their kindness to Carinthia—the eccentric Crœsus sets up in a Piccadilly fruit-shop. Indeed, on further reflection, "he grew so far reconciled to her [Carinthia] as to have intimation of a softness coming on"; his past conduct, "so justifiable then, as he forced himself to think," seemed now hideous. But his pride still prevents him from seeing all his past misdeeds and his present duty, whilst Carinthia's association with the former is actually set down to her discredit.

Meanwhile Carinthia also had slowly awakened. She is convinced that her husband hated her ; otherwise his conduct is inexplicable. The birth of her child naturally roused a new sense of dread and antagonism, since both child and mother would now be "under perpetual menace from an unscrupulous tyrannical man." For herself, Carinthia cared little now. "Sure of her rectitude, a stranger to the world, she was not very sensible of dishonour done to her name." But on behalf of her child and her brother, who now absorb all her affection, she would welcome a treaty of peace with Lord Fleet-

George Meredith

wood. "I am spared loving him when I forgive him ; and I do. The loving is the pain. That is gone by." When a strike among the miners induces Lord Fleetwood to send down Kit Ines to protect Carinthia and her child, she, mindful of a former experience, fears this is an attempt to kidnap the child, and so withdraws to the house of a neighbouring mine-owner, Mr. Owain Wythan, who had chanced to be at the prize-fight on her wedding-day. His invalid wife is one of her staunchest friends, and to him Carinthia is "Morgana le Fay Christianised."* Gower Woodseer, to whom his lordship has become reconciled, is then despatched to persuade her to withdraw from Wales to Esslemont. But his errand is in vain. Designs upon the child are still suspected, and Gower remains to fall in love with

* The subtle point of this allusion (ch. xxix) is that in Boiardo's "Orlando Innamorato" the beautiful and enchanting Morgana punishes Orlando, who has failed to seize his opportunity, by eluding for a while his pursuit ; in his quest of her, he is scourged by "La Penitenza," and warned against carelessly losing his prize even when he has secured it. The relevant passages are worked into the plot of Peacock's "Gryll Grange " (chs. xx—xxiv) ; already in "Beauchamp's Career" Meredith had reterred to Boiardo and his later adapter, Berni. To Owain, the relations of Carinthia and Lord Fleetwood seem to resemble those of Morgana and her tardily awakened lover.

The Amazing Marriage

Madge and see "the priceless woman whom Lord Fleetwood could call wife fast slipping away from him." Despite his stiff reluctance to meet her, the Earl at last arrives, partly to settle the strike, partly through a cold curiosity to see his child or rather "the male infant of such a mother," partly through an irrepressible feeling of attraction for Carinthia which he is puzzled and half-ashamed to own. She is at least unique, he confesses, and "the wealthy young nobleman prized any form of rareness wherever it was visible." Possibly even she had something to forgive, he admits. But certainly, he recollects, his injustice to her is more excusable than the grotesque ridicule with which she had covered them both.

Apologising thus for himself, and making his very imperfect penitence a means of securing his dignity and pleasure, the Earl is disgusted to find himself actually suspected of designs upon the child. Carinthia's suspicions —for she had never complained or condescended to speak of injuries—are a new outrage to his pride. Her absence from the castle is construed as a personal insult. Hence, in spite of some plain-speaking from

George Meredith

Gower, he refuses to see her and prepares for instant departure. "Capable of villainy as of nobility," he swings back to the former. When Carinthia calmly ("like a lance in air") appears next day with her child to bid him farewell and consult him on the boy's name, he curtly rejects her appeal for an allowance of money, orders her to live at Esslemont, and looks at her child as hastily as he would kick a stone in his path. The climax of her offence is furnished by her bravery in protecting him, at the risk of her own life, from a mad dog, and by her fruitless attempt to persuade a Welsh mother to have her bitten child cauterised. Her courage made him feel small and eclipsed, even while he was forced to admit her coolness. Yet "courage to grapple with his pride and open his heart was wanting in him." Assuming a lordly indifference, though he secretly felt obscured and was wrathful alike at the feeling and at the woman who stirred it, the Earl drove away to rejoin his yachting party at Cardiff. Again his warmer feelings of admiration and respect for Carinthia—for unlike Othello he has stray thoughts that ebb back

384

to love—had been chilled by his proud dread of subjection and the disappointment to his hope of finding her gratefully submissive to his superior authority.

Two months later, Rebecca Wythan's death sets Carinthia free to journey South to Esslemont. But this act of tardy submission is a source of fresh irritation to her husband. In her honour, and to prevent any risk of the child being kidnapped, nine Welsh gentlemen, headed by Mr. Wythan, act as her escort to Kent, a proceeding which the Earl wrathfully regards as pantomimic and gratuitous. (Meredith introduces at this point a characteristically Rabelaisian account of a drinking-bout, ch. xxxiv.) He suspects her of trying to dominate him or to make him ridiculous, and he will not listen to Woodseer's explanation that her dread of the child being kidnapped is physiologically due to her own capture and imprisonment during her pregnancy. Exasperation irrationally drives him once more to the device of perverting Henrietta and feeding on her humiliation, while he also lets Kit Ines use foul play in order to prevent Chillon winning a wager at

Y

athletics. Chillon had undertaken the wager
to get money, and it was to help her brother
that Carinthia really wished an allowance
from her husband. Thus by stinting her and
cheating him, he imagined his revenge
complete. But Carinthia has well-founded
suspicions of his treachery in regard to
Chillon ; and when he goes down to visit her
for the first time at Esslemont, his reception
is as chilly as the March day on which they
meet. When he arrives, she is absent at
Croridge on a visit to her brother, who has
been forced to sell out of the army for money
to pay his debts and support Henrietta. When
she does appear, it is with Mr. Wythan, whom
(at his wife's dying request) she calls by his
first name. Her own term for himself, "my
lord," is a rude change from the earlier
"my husband," which he had once resented,
and which, since his conduct in London, she
had finally dropped. He makes a weak
attempt, not to apologise, but to regain his
hold of her, but his tardy offer of money is
now rejected, since Chillon's need for it
(thanks to his own intrigue) is gone. Lastly,
his proposal to spend the night is met by the

blunt, defensive, significant phrase, "I guard my rooms." The moody young earl drives away, divided between respect for the strength of character which extorted his reluctant admiration, and furious anger at her quiet disdain of what he considers to have been his undeserved generosity. Respect on the whole prevails. By an ironic accident, he finds himself obliged to spend the night at the very inn where he had abandoned Carinthia on her honeymoon, and this helps to warn the fool of what he is doing.

Jealousy of Lord Brailstone, who is flirting with Henrietta in his absence, almost throws him off the line again. But he is steadied by the suicide of one of his sycophants or Ixionides (as Gower termed them) through losses at gambling and a *penchant* for Livia. In a fluctuation of passion, he resolves to settle the latter lady with a handsome income, conditional on her marriage, and to establish Carinthia at the head of the forthcoming entertainments at Calesford which he had promised to give in honour of Henrietta. Woodseer is employed as the envoy; but, while he manages for himself to win Madge's

George Meredith

heart, his mission to Carinthia is a failure.
Apart from the injuries done to herself, she
cannot forgive Lord Fleetwood for his
treachery to her brother. Thus at last the
luckless Earl begins to see that " there 's not
an act of a man's life lies dead behind him, but
it is blessing or cursing him every step he
takes." Most of the Earl's acts, in his ill-
assorted relationship with Carinthia, are
cursing him now. Her arctic, courteous,
dignified behaviour punishes and vexes him
cruelly. His own appeals, his tardy fits of
partial penitence ("I was possessed! sort of
were-wolf!"), produce no impression, for
Carinthia inherits from her father a stern
aversion to the weakness of forgiving an
injury, and she bluntly tells him that her
heart is given now to her brother and her
child. By a strange fatality, they part at the
graveyard of the church in which they had
been married. She turns from him, promising
to honour the marriage-tie and yet refusing
any further relations with himself, till the
Earl, now in a lover's mood, as he watches
her vanish, fears she may be lost to him. For
his egotistic soul is distressed rather by what

he is losing in her than by what she has suffered from him.

Yet another effort, however, he will make to regain her. Thanks to the varied influences of Lord Feltre and Woodseer, he is beginning to waken "to the claims of others—youth's infant conscience," and actually to the need and duty of doing some penance to his injured wife, if ever he is to be clean again or to win back her affection. He is haunted by the apposite saying, "half of our funny heathen lives we are bent double to gather things we have tossed away." In this enterprise of gathering he secures an interview with Carinthia and Chillon. The latter, thanks to Lord Fleetwood's underhand intrigue at the athletic contest, is now forced to gratify his soldiering instinct by taking service in the English contingent of the Spanish army, and as Carinthia, who prefers to accompany him, is in any case indignant at the treatment of her brother, the poor Earl thus finds himself hoist by his own petard. His attempts to apologise to Carinthia are spoiled by two flaws. In the first place, his pride will not stoop to that complete exposure of himself which probably

George Meredith

would have stirred brother and sister to some compassion. He feels the degradation of confession more than the degradation of what has to be confessed, and in the cowardice of pride he hesitates to strip himself bare. Further, his intercourse with Lord Feltre had fostered the sentimental delusion that such extreme penitential acts are due from men to the priest only. With his ethical sense thus impaired, he naturally fails to persuade Carinthia and Chillon of his sincerity ; he is quietly tried, judged, and put aside, after a tardy and imperfect disavowal of his pride. Unaware of any conflict, Carinthia wrestled with him, "flung him, pitied him, and passed on along her path elsewhere."

Thereupon Lord Fleetwood, after a rupture with Lord Brailstone, dallies with the alternative:—his wife or Rome (to the consternation of Protestant society). Having apparently forfeited his manhood, he will take refuge in monasticism. Lord Levellier's death frees Chillon from monetary embarrassments, but he is still bent on Spain, and Carinthia is divided between the plan of accompanying him and the duty of remaining at home to be

The Amazing Marriage

with the weak, flighty, Henrietta, who will
not accompany her infatuated and indulgent
husband to the scene of war. Chillon
persuades his sister to remain, hinting at
the possibility and advisability of some compromise with her husband. She herself
retains some slight emotion of pity for the
weak young nobleman. But in their final
interview his pride again blinds him to the
fact that his one chance lies in complete,
immediate confession, and in confession to
Carinthia instead of to a priest. "In spite of
horror, the task of helping to wash a black
soul white would have been her compensation
for loss of companionship with her soldier
brother. She would have held hot iron to
the rabid wound, and come to a love of the
rescued sufferer." Carinthia, in short, was in
a mood melting to union and reconciliation
with her husband. But, with the tactlessness
of pride, he failed to use his opportunity.
Nor did he get another. The crisis is pre-
cipitated by an outburst of jealous passion on
Lord Brailstone's part, which suddenly reveals
to Henrietta Lord Fleetwood's previous
intrigue against herself. She flies to her

George Meredith

sister-in-law for protection, and this discovery of her husband's additional villainy finally destroys Carinthia's inclination towards him. His guilt absolves her from any further dealings with him. She and Henrietta at once proceed to Spain. Returning two years later, she finds that Lord Fleetwood has become a Roman Catholic monk; after his death, she fulfils Rebecca Wythan's dying wish and marries Owain, who thus, like the staunch Redworth, at last wins the rare pearl which a base Indian, "richer than all his tribe," had flung away and tried, when it was too late, to recover.

Lord Fleetwood is the conventional young man of society, whose wealth makes him think he can buy anything, even a woman. Meredith has satirized this plutocratic view of life in "The Empty Purse," where he attacks the aristocrat's abuse of money to indulge his passions.

"Thereanon the keen passions clapped wing,
    Fixed eye, and the world was prey. . . .
    And O the grace of his air,
    As he at the goblet sips,
    A centre of girdles loosed,
    With their grisly label, sold."

392

The Amazing Marriage

This ideal of woman* is fostered by Fleetwood's experience of the Countess Livia, and the cynical, eccentric peer makes the mistake of treating Carinthia as one of the crowd. Meredith develops this favourite theme with gusto, but also with a minuteness and a wealth of illustration which become almost wearisome.

The scene (in ch. xi) in which Lord Fleetwood first sees Carinthia poised daringly on a tree, should be compared with the similar scene, of which it is evidently a reminiscence and adaptation, in Peacock's "Crotchet Castle" (ch. xviii), where also the lover's passion is kindled by his first glimpse of the self-possessed heroine (like Carinthia, a lover of the mountains) calmly and gracefully seated on a tree overhanging a cataract.

The Carlist war in Spain, referred to in ch. xliii, is not the insurrection of Don Carlos against Queen Christina (1834—1840), when a British corps was raised by Sir De Lacy Evans and other soldiers in aid of her Majesty, but the later insurrection by General

---

* There is a prose version of it in the 55th chapter of "The Adventures of Harry Richmond" : "his (i.e. Heriot's) talk of women still suggested the hawk with the downy feathers of the last little plucked bird sticking to his beak."

George Meredith

O'Donnell in favour of the Queen during 1841—1843, which centred in the Pyrenees. As Carinthia left for Spain with Chillon in the year after her child's birth, the amazing marriage cannot therefore have been much later than 1839, when Chillon was twenty-four years of age. Reckoning back from this we reach 1814 as the time when Captain Kirby eloped with his Countess, and this synchronises with the data of the opening chapter which describes the presence of a Russian Emperor in London, after a long period of warfare. It was in the early summer of 1814 that Alexander I of Russia visited this country, after the surrender of Paris to the Allies and the collapse of Napoleon.

Several characteristics of Meredith's craft reappear throughout this novel. The racy, pungent sayings from the old Buccaneer's "Book of Maxims for Men" correspond to those from the "Pilgrim's Scrip" in "The Ordeal of Richard Feverel." The device of introducing the tale with a cloud of gossip is employed in the opening chapter of "Diana," whilst the cognate use of ballads is familiar to readers of "Chloe." But all through the

The Amazing Marriage

present novel Meredith uses Dame Gossip (in whose name the first three chapters are written) as an occasion for introducing his repeated defence of the analytic, introspective element in a story of character; see chapters xiii, xx, xxxv, xxxviii, and the closing paragraph of the novel. The style is not tainted at many points with Meredithese; the "sensational shanks" and "vertiginous roast haunch" are, on the whole, exceptional.

For a comparative study of the novelist, it may be observed that the fine passage in ch. xxviii (beginning: "Now to the Cymry and to the pure Kelt, the past is at their elbows continually") corresponds to an earlier passage in "One of Our Conquerors" (ch. xi, beginning: "The Kelts, as they are called, can't and won't forgive injuries"); and that Chillon's sole apology for Lord Fleetwood's rascally conduct ("he had never been thrashed," ch. xlvii) echoes the favourite Meredithian principle enunciated most decisively by Dr. Middleton in "The Egoist" (ch. ix). Some hints for the sketch of Gower Woodseer, it has been conjectured, were taken from the character of Robert Louis Stevenson.

George Meredith

Meredith makes him the exponent of a healthy Open Road philosophy, but at one point (ch. xxv) he describes him as "a young man studying abstract and adoring surface nature too exclusively to be aware of the manifestation of her spirit in the flesh." This is a significant touch. For Nature in Meredith's scheme of life includes human nature, as appears in the "Earth's Secret" and "The Thrush in February" especially.

Pride and sentimentalism are, as usual, the forces of mischief in the "Amazing Marriage." The latter is the key to Henrietta's romantic, emotional, shallow soul. The former predominates in Lord Fleetwood's complex character, which sways between the dog and the gentleman, the devil and the cherub; it is developed through his relations with women, and these bring out its latent weakness, as they exhibit the secret fibre of Woodseer's nature. Great wealth, with the opportunity of gratifying his whims, fosters in the earl an autocratic spirit which demands submission to its will as the condition of experiencing its generosity. This forms the cause of his moral disaster. Accustomed to

396

The Amazing Marriage

luxurious dependants on his bounty, like Livia, he misreads Carinthia's nobler soul, and Meredith makes him an example of how a man's attitude to women is bound up with his view of Nature. Between the brainless Lord Feltre's Catholic conception of women as "devil's bait,"essentially a snare and hindrance to man's purity, and Lord Fleetwood's cynical use or abuse of the sex as toys, Gower Woodseer presents the sane Meredithian philosophy of a frank, healthy attitude of respect towards women as neither Lesbias nor Beatrices. Lord Fleetwood has his sentimental impulses, as is shown by his purchase of the greengrocer's shop where Carinthia once had stayed, and by his final lapse into monasticism. But these are not necessarily moral. They can exist alongside of shiftiness, cruelty, and obstinacy, and indeed it is his pride that ultimately ruins him by obtaining the ascendancy over his better impulses.

Livia belongs to the unpleasant sisterhood of Mrs. Lovell in "Rhoda Fleming." On the other hand, Mrs. Wythan recalls Lady Dunstane, and the stout-hearted, loyal, comely Madge Winch (Gower's "flower among grass-blades"), with her devotion to Carinthia, forms one of the most attractive figures in Meredith's series of minor female characters. Carinthia herself is not so lovable as women like Diana, Nataly Radnor, and Vittoria. The more passive circumstances of her marriage offer less scope for her development than in the case of Mrs. Warwick. But Meredith has given her in rich measure the charm of womanliness and mettle, of sensitiveness knit to courage, and of an unspoiled, calm strength of character which only ripens through ill-treatment. Like Aminta, this superb woman is left by her lord to the world, and she remains pure ; although the course of the two women is widely different, their sheen is untarnished by temptations. Cruelty drives neither to mawkish pathos or self-assertion. In Carinthia's case the bitter discipline is successfully endured through her hereditary nerve and native seriousness, whilst the "sad and ripe corage" of her soul is developed through motherhood and deep affection for her brother into something higher than Griselda's gentle patience.

The psychological interest of the novel lies in its treatment of the two leading characters,

The Amazing Marriage

with Henrietta as a foil to Carinthia, and Woodseer as a relief to Lord Fleetwood. But Carinthia, Madge, and Woodseer are the vital figures of the tale. The hero (?) is exaggerated to the point of unreality. Despite his friendships with Gower and Lord Feltre, he really is influenced, like Edward Blancove, by the tone of his society associates, whilst like draws to like in the intercourse of the Wythans and Madge with Carinthia. The writer's descriptive power shows no falling off in the passages on the mountain-scenery of the Black Forest district (ch. iv-v), and the prize-fight (ch. xvi), to say nothing of the portrait of Charles Dump (ch. ii), the old Buccaneer's postillion, which, like the smaller sketches in "Diana" (ch. xi), and "Lord Ormont,"* calls up vividly the atmosphere of the stage-coaching days in pre-Victorian England.

---

* There is another parallel. Sir Walter Scott was convinced "that no schoolmaster whatsoever has existed, without his having some private reserve of extreme absurdity"—an opinion, by the way, which is as reasonable as his estimate of journalists. In "Lord Ormont" it looks as if Meredith took the schoolmaster as hero, in order to brush aside such conventional prejudices. Weyburn shows Lord Ormont how to behave, and, in his own way, Woodseer, the son of a dissenting minister, reads Lord Fleetwood a proper lesson upon how gentlemen should conduct themselves towards women. The aristocrats in both cases behave, in Mr. Le Gallienne's phrase, "with that studied brutality for which no one can match an English aristocrat."

Index

Index

402

Index